PENGUIN PASSNOTES

The Rime of the Ancient Mariner *and Other Narrative Poems*

Dr Stephen Coote was educated at Magdalene College, Cambridge, where he was an exhibitioner, and at Birkbeck College, University of London, where he was Sir William Bull Memorial Scholar. After a period teaching and working as an examiner in English literature, he was principal of tutorial colleges in both Oxford and London. He has written a number of books for Penguins and, in particular, is General Editor of the Penguin Passnotes series and joint General Editor of the Penguin Masterstudies in English Literature.

PENGUIN PASSNOTES

The Rime of the Ancient Mariner
and Other Narrative Poems

STEPHEN COOTE, M.A., PH.D.

PENGUIN BOOKS

Penguin Books Ltd, Harmondsworth, Middlesex, England
Viking Penguin Inc., 40 West 23rd Street, New York, New York 10010, U.S.A.
Penguin Books Australia Ltd, Victoria, Australia
Penguin Books Canada Limited, 2801 John Street, Markham, Ontario, Canada L3R 1B4
Penguin Books (N.Z.) Ltd, 182–190 Wairau Road, Auckland 10, New Zealand

First published 1986

Copyright © Stephen Coote, 1986
All rights reserved

Made and printed in Great Britain by
Richard Clay (The Chaucer Press) Ltd, Bungay, Suffolk
Filmset in 10/12 pt Monophoto Ehrhardt by
Northumberland Press Ltd, Gateshead, Tyne and Wear

Except in the United States of America, this book is sold subject
to the condition that it shall not, by way of trade or otherwise, be lent,
re-sold, hired out, or otherwise circulated without the
publisher's prior consent in any form of binding or cover other than
that in which it is published and without a similar condition
including this condition being imposed on the subsequent purchaser

*The publishers are grateful to the following Examination Boards
for permission to reproduce questions from examination papers:*
University of Oxford Delegacy of Local Examinations
University of London Schools Examinations Board

Contents

To the Student	6
Introduction	7
The Ballads: *Sir Patrick Spens*	9
Edom O'Gordon	10
Jock o' the Side	12
Edward, Edward	14
The Unquiet Grave	16
The Wife of Usher's Well	16
Thomas the Rhymer	16
John Gilpin	18
Peter Grimes	22
Michael	31
The Rime of the Ancient Mariner	37
The Eve of St Agnes	57
Morte d'Arthur	68
Sohrab and Rustum	73
The Sacrilege	83
Lepanto	86
Themes and Characters: *Landscapes, Seascapes, etc*	91
Love	98
Crime and Punishment	106
War	109
Parents and Children	113
Poetic Language and Forms	115
Glossary	121
Examination Questions	125

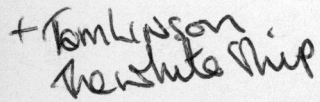

To the Student

This book is designed to help you with your O-level, C.S.E. or G.C.S.E. English Literature examinations. It contains an introduction to narrative verse, an analysis of a number of poems and a commentary on some of the issues raised by the texts.

When you use this book remember that it is no more than an aid to your study. It will help you find passages quickly and perhaps give you some ideas for essays. But remember also: *This book is not a substitute for reading the poems, and it is your knowledge and your response that matter.* These are the things that the examiners are looking for, and they are also the things that will give you the most pleasure. Show your knowledge and appreciation to the examiner, and show them clearly.

Introduction

A narrative poem is one that tells a story. This definition seems simple enough yet it hardly does justice to the wide range of poetry we shall be discussing in this volume. Some of the works we shall be considering are comic – *John Gilpin* and *Jock o' the Side* are examples of these – while others will show us a whole range of emotions from guilt and shame, crime and punishment, heroism and tragedy, to rapturous human passion. If narrative poems present us with vivid and varied plots, it is clear that they are also capable of leading us into an exploration of some of the most exciting emotional states.

At the heart of all these poems lies a concern for the experiences that imagined men and women can go through. Deeper than the surface excitement of the story is an interest in what we are: how we love and hate, disobey and are punished, are brave or cowardly, lucky or trapped in tragic circumstances. If we begin to examine these areas, letting our feelings slowly come to understand what the poets are presenting us with, we shall also come to see that the works discussed here offer the widest range of human experience.

The poems also cover a great span of time and a considerable variety of different verse forms. Some of the poems – the ballads, for example – are ancient pieces. Others, like *John Gilpin*, and *Peter Grimes* come from the eighteenth century. You may like to contrast these two works to see how the same age could produce such very different pictures of its world. Perhaps the greatest poems we shall be discussing come from the early nineteenth century, from what is known as the age of the Romantics. As we might expect, love and imagination are crucial here. In *The Rime of the Ancient Mariner* we are asked to stretch our imaginations to the fullest in order to appreciate Coleridge's discussion of the importance of love for all living things. In *The Eve of St Agnes* Keats again kindles our intuitions so that we can appreciate the splendours of human passion. In Wordsworth's *Michael* we are asked to see how a failure of love and imagination leads to a young man's destruction and his father's despair.

The range of verse forms the poets use is also very wide. The ballads appear simple but are truly powerful. *Peter Grimes* is written in highly contrived couplets and yet presents us with a wild despair. *The Rime of the Ancient Mariner* re-uses the form of the ballads, while the work of two Victorian poets – Matthew Arnold and Tennyson – employs perhaps the most common form of English verse, the iambic pentameter line with its five stressed syllables alternating with five unstressed ones.

If, as you read these poems, you keep in mind this variety of moods and methods, the powerful analyses of human passion and the sheer excitement of the works, not only will you be introduced to some new and important literature but you will begin to see how a poem which, on the surface, appears only to tell a story, in fact can offer a penetrating analysis of the ways in which we live.

The Ballads

Nobody knows who the authors of these powerful, doom-laden poems were. They are anonymous. It is also far from certain when the works were written. Some of them are very old indeed and may well come from the Middle Ages. The so-called Border Ballads are definitely ancient pieces. Despite their name many of them appear to have been composed in north-west Scotland; but, again, their precise origin is uncertain. All we do know is that their authors were poets of the very highest standing, and that they almost certainly did not write these poems down. They are oral works which were communicated by word of mouth and learnt by heart. They were almost certainly sung.

Sir Patrick Spens is one of the finest of the Border Ballads. Note how simply and vividly it creates its effects. We see the King sitting in Dunfermline 'drinking the blude-red wine'. The wine certainly suggests festivities, but the fact that it is blood-red already alerts us to the death that will so quickly sweep over the characters in the poem.

The King then calls for 'a skeely skipper' to sail his new ship. Only in stanza IV are we informed that the purpose of the voyage is to bring back from Norway a royal bride for the Scottish king. One of the courtiers nominates Sir Patrick Spens to be captain of the ship. We are told that 'Sir Patrick Spens is the best sailor/That ever sail'd the sea'.

With the speed of action that is characteristic of the Border Ballads, stanza III tells us how the King writes a long letter to Sir Patrick. Amazement, fear and sorrow strike at the good man's heart as he paces along the seashore. He believes that he has been tricked into making a voyage that will certainly result in his death.

> O wha is this has done this deed
>   And tauld the king o' me,
> To send us out, at this time o' year,
>   To sail upon the sea?

The winter sea between Scotland and Norway is utterly treacherous and yet the absolute allegiance that Sir Patrick owes to his king means that he must cross it, braving storms and disaster in his romantic mission. Briefly and powerfully, several strong emotions are thrown together: love, duty, fear and loyalty. The poet wastes no words and yet, in a little over twenty-five lines, he has managed to convey to us a whole world.

The eighth stanza describes the ship setting out and, although the next verse begins with exclamations of encouragement from Sir Patrick, these are immediately followed by a sense of doom and death. No sooner has Sir Patrick spoken than one of his sailors declares, 'I fear a deadly storm'. We know at once that Sir Patrick's initial fear and horror were wholly justified. We also know that the whole voyage will be a disaster. The tenth stanza with its image of the new moon encircling the old offers a dreadful omen. Once more, with the ruthless speed that characterizes the poem, we hear of the onslaught of the storm. Like everything else in the poem, it is violent, sudden and deadly: the little boat is smashed to pieces. In stanza XIII we hear Sir Patrick desperately asking for a sailor to take the helm while he climbs the topmast to see if he can spy land. A loyal sailor offers to take the helm but tells Sir Patrick that even if he climbs to the top of the tallest mast he will never spy land. Now, amid doom and despair, the boat begins to flood. At first, with the experience of true sailors, the men try to cover over the rent in the ship's side with cloth. They use the expensive fabric designed as a gift for the King of Norway, 'But still the sea came in'.

The Scots lords are reluctant to soil their ridiculously fashionable clothes but, as the poem tells us, they are soon to drown anyway. Their hats become soaked and their gorgeous apparel floats away on the water. The image of their destruction is dreadful. The poet tells us, 'And mony was the gude lord's son/That never mair cam hame'. Then, with the speed and dramatic contrasts which characterize all the ballads, the poet tells us of how the women who love these courtiers will never see them again. Stanzas XX and XXI give us a picture both of beauty and of great sadness. Sir Patrick and the lords who sailed with him on the fatal expedition to win the Scots king his bride lie fifty fathoms under the treacherous water.

Edom O'Gordon is a savage tale of border warfare. The opening stanzas describe how the hero, Edom, needs to find a place in which to shelter during the winter. We may assume that he has spent the earlier part of the year raiding and pillaging. He decides to go to 'the house o' the Rodes'. He chooses this place because of the 'fair ladye' who lives there. With the rapid changes we have seen to be typical of the ballads, we are then introduced to the lady herself. She is looking down from her castle walls and sees a host of men riding towards her. She asks her servants if they can see them too. In stanza V we learn that the lady of Rodes believes the men to be her husband and his followers returning home. The poet tells us that this is not so:

> It was the traitor, Edom o' Gordon,
> Wha reck'd nae sin nor shame.

We learn for the first time the true nature of Edom. He is clearly a violent and wicked man, and in the next stanza we are told that he has surrounded the fortifications of the house of Rodes. The terrified lady of the house runs up to the tower and, in a desperate attempt to save herself, tries to pacify Edom. He will have none of it. He begs the lady to come down to him for he wishes to seduce her. In stanza X the repetition emphasizes the defiance of the lady, but we surely feel that she is no match for her enemy. However, her words have angered him and he orders her to surrender the house. If she does not do so, he will burn her and her 'babies three' to death.

Still the lady defies him and she bids her servant bring her a pistol. We must imagine her standing terrified at the top of the tower looking down at the fierce marauder and his men, in the greatest peril. She fires the gun twice but she misses 'that bluidy butcher's heart'. The furious Edom now orders that the house be razed to the ground. His amorous longing for the lady turns to desire for vicious revenge.

But Edom is not the only danger the lady confronts, for there is a traitor in her castle. Despite having looked after him and regularly paid his wages, her man Jock is a turncoat and has become one of Edom's followers. It is Jock who betrays the castle and allows Edom to set fire to it. As the castle begins to burn, so the lady's little son, sitting on his nurse's knee, begins to complain about the reek of smoke. The lady declares she would do anything to protect him from this. Her little daughter then speaks up. She asks to be wrapped in a pair of sheets and thrown over the castle wall, perhaps to safety. The servants wrap the little girl as she has asked and throw her over the castle wall, but, far from falling to safety, she lands on the point of Edom's spear and dies. Stanza XXIII is a short but vivid portrayal of her girlish beauty and her death. Even Edom is moved by these. As he turns her body over and sees her face, so moved is he by her beauty that he says she is the first person that he wishes would come back to life. Indeed, he continues to turn her over and over, staring at her white skin. The horror of her death evidently moves even this villain. He realizes what a beautiful wife she would have made if she had been allowed to grow up. So horrified is Edom by the sight of the little girl's corpse that he bids his men 'busk and boun' – in other words, get ready to go. In some primitive way Edom feels that the death of the girl can only bring him and his men bad luck. He cannot bear to look on 'that bonnie face' of the body lying in the grass.

One of Edom's men is horrified at his master's superstitions. In stanza XXVII he tells him that whoever concerns himself about 'freits' or omens will surely be hounded by such things. In other words, he tells Edom that if he is superstitious the bad luck that he fears will indeed be his. Let it never be said, the man declares, that Edom O'Gordon was 'daunted by a dame'.

The next stanza returns us to the burning castle, to the weeping lady, her children and their certainty that they will be burnt to death. The castle is burning around them and Edom again declares that it is time for him and his marauding men to ride away. At this moment the lady's husband arrives. As he nears his home so he sees that it is burning down. The horror of the sight pierces his heart and he tells his men to ride on as fast as they may. His loyal troops ride or run as fast as they can, but it is too late. By the time that they arrive at the house of Rodes 'Baith lady and babes were brent'. The lard of Rodes chases Gordon, eventually catches up with him and revenges the death of the lady 'i' the Gordon's foul heart's blude'.

This is a savage and dreadful tale of action and violent feelings. Notice how the terse language and verse form help to produce these effects.

Jock o' the Side is another ballad concerned with a border raid; but on this occasion, although it starts with death and disaster, it ends on a happy and even comic note. The Lord of Liddesdale has led a raid against the English, but Michael o' Winfield has been killed and his son Jock taken prisoner. This news comes to Sybill o' the Side, the wife of the dead man and the mother of the hero of the poem. She rushes immediately to her brother, Mangerton, to tell him what has happened. With the terseness characteristic of these ballads, stanza IV describes the grief with which the news is greeted. Mangerton vows to save Jock from certain death at the hands of the English. He calls on three of his stoutest men to help him: 'the Laird's Jock', 'the Laird's Wat' and 'Hobbie Noble', an English traitor whose dreadful misdeeds have forced him to go over to the side of the Scots. Lord Mangerton then proceeds to unfold a clever plan. The horses of the three men will be shod the wrong way round so that anybody looking at the traces left in the earth will be misled by them. He also tells them to disguise themselves, to hide their armour under their countryman's clothing.

When this is done the three men set off. Stanza XII describes how, by the light of the moon, they cut down a tree which they hope to use as a ladder to scale the walls of Newcastle where Jock is held prisoner. However, when they arrive at the town they find that the tree is too short for their purpose and so, being brave, foolhardy men, they decide to use the tree trunk as a battering ram and smash through the town gates. They break the neck of the guard or 'porter' who has been trying to resist their entry, and then make straight for the jail.

They call out to Jock who, despairing of his life, mournfully asks who these people are that they know his name. 'The gude laird's Jock' tells the prisoner who the company are, but the jailed man declares that they will never be able to free him. Besides, he is to die the following morning. A heavy weight of 'Spanish iron' has been fastened to Jock to hold him safely in the prison, while the dark and dreary dungeon itself is securely locked. The Laird's Jock tells him not to worry about this, saying 'A faint heart ne'er wan a fair ladie'. He vows that they will free the prisoner, and indeed they do. They smash the doors to splinters and the mighty Laird's Jock picks up the prisoner – Spanish iron and all – throws him over his shoulder and carries him down the stairs of the tolbooth. Hobbie Noble, the Englishman, is amazed at the Scotsman's strength, but the powerful hero only laughs and declares that Jock o' the Side is lighter than a flea. When the four men have safely fled the town, they place the freed prisoner on a horse but, because of the iron with which he is fettered, he is forced to sit side-saddle, like a woman. The Laird's Jock teases him about this. They ride on until they get to Cholerton ford, the place where they had cut down the tree trunk which they used as a battering ram. They ask an old man if it is safe for them to ford the water at this point, and are told that this is quite impossible. The Laird's 'saft Wat', the most cowardly man in the company, declares that there is nothing for them to do but die in that case. Obviously they are being pursued by men from Newcastle, and when these men catch up with them they will certainly be outnumbered. The Laird's 'ain Jock' scorns such cowardice and defiantly leads the group of men as they wade across the ford.

They arrive safely on the other side and no sooner have they done so than the party of twenty men sent out from Newcastle to arrest them comes into sight. The officer in charge – lacking the heroic resolve of the Scots – declares that the ford is impassable. He pathetically and rather amusingly calls out to the Scots and tells them to take their prisoner by all means, but at least leave him the fetters, the fifteen stone of Spanish iron with which Jock has been encumbered. Once again the Laird's 'ain Jock' hurls his defiance. He will certainly not leave the fetters behind. He will keep them and shoe his horses with them.

Safe on the other side of the ford, the company rides away to safety and we last see them sitting by the warmth, comfort and safety of their fireside drinking and reflecting that the past day was supposed to see Jock o' the Side hanged.

Edward, Edward is perhaps the most sinister and gruesome of all the ballads and certainly one of the most powerful. It is a confrontation between a young aristocrat and his mother in which the woman slowly wrings from her son the confession that he has murdered his father. Notice how the repetition of the young man's name 'Edward, Edward' and of his phrase 'mither, mither' subtly increase the tension.

The mother asks why Edward's sword is dropping with blood. Immediately we imagine him standing in front of her with the sign of his guilt all too evident. At first he lies to her, claiming rather pathetically that he has killed his hawk. The mother's response is both subtle and cruel. She does not say directly that her son is lying but simply declares 'Your hawk's blude was never sae red'. She is clearly enjoying watching the young man's suffering. Again, he tries to lie, declaring that he has killed his horse, and that she was 'sae fair and free'. This excuse is not good enough either. The sadistic mother is clearly enjoying the torture she is inflicting and declares that Edward's horse was old and that, anyway, he has others. The mounting pain is almost unbearable. Edward at last confesses his crime:

> I hae kill'd my father dear,
>   Mither, mither;
> O I hae kill'd my father dear,
>   Alas, and wae is me, O!'

His mother's cold, hard nature again asserts its ruthlessness. She says nothing about the deed itself, nothing about her own feelings and nothing at all about the murdered man. She merely increases Edward's anguish by asking him what penance he will do for the murder he has committed. He tells her that he will sail away from the country. Again, his mother finds in his answer a further means of torturing him. What will the young man do with his fine house when he has fled away? The suggestion is that he will find life mean and wretched without his wealth and his home. The young man's answer – and perhaps we should imagine him spitting out these words in his defiance – is a bitter one. He declares that he will let them stand where they will till they fall down in ruins. Again the mother is quite unmoved. Her delight lies, as always, in increasing the young man's torture. She has made him confess, she has told him that he will have to undergo penance, she has told him that if he runs away his life will be wretched without his possessions. Now she asks him how his wife and children will survive without him. The young man's guilt rises to an hysterical pitch. So intense is his suffering, his feeling of remorse, that for the moment he denies all responsibility for his family. With defiant bitterness he hurls his answer at his mother:

> The warld's room: let them beg through life,
>   Mither, mither;
> The warld's room: let them beg through life;
>   For them never mair will I see, O.

The young man's mother has removed all his supports. She has exposed the raw nerve of his guilt, watching him writhe in emotional anguish as she does so. Finally, in the last stanza, she refers to herself. She asks Edward what he will leave to her now that he is going into exile. His answer is one of terrible savagery:

> The curse of hell frae me sall ye bear,
> Mither, mither;
> The curse of hell frae me sall ye bear:
> Sic counsels ye gave to me, O!

In a poem whose tension has mounted stanza by stanza, it is only in the last line that the full and dreadful truth is revealed. It is the mother herself who ordered Edward to kill his father, her own husband. We shiver in horror as we realize the full depths of this woman's depravity, she who has not only urged her son to murder his father but has enjoyed extracting his terrible confession from him, syllable by syllable.

Not all the ballads are concerned with violence and bloodshed. Some of them deal with love, though this often assumes a sinister air. *The Unquiet Grave*, for example, deals with the despair of a young man whose sweetheart has died. Her ghost comes to him and informs him that if she gives him the kiss he craves he too will soon die. She tells him that it would be far better for him to make the best of his life until God calls him. Again, *The Wife of Usher's Well* is about ghosts and tells him how the spirits of three dead sons appear to their elderly mother and then disappear at daybreak. Magic, indeed, is one of the great themes of the ballads and, of all those that deal with fairyland, *Thomas the Rhymer* is perhaps the finest.

It is a tale about a poet and describes the magic and infatuation of a poet's love. It opens with a description of the Queen of Fairyland – a bewitchingly beautiful woman – as she approaches Thomas. He immediately raises his cap to her, kneels down and declares that the woman is so beautiful that she must be the Virgin Mary. She is forced to deny this:

> 'O no, O no, Thomas,' she said,
> 'That name does not belang to me;
> I'm but the Queen o' fair Elfland,
> That am hither come to visit thee.'

And she has come for a purpose. She knows that she can bewitch Thomas. She tells him that if he dares to kiss her he will be completely in her power. Thomas, of course, immediately gives her the kiss and she declares that he will have to go with her and be her servant for seven years.

How powerfully the poem gives the impression of a fine man utterly enthralled by the magical power of a beautiful woman. Thomas is wholly infatuated by her. She takes him up on her 'milk-white steed' and rides off with him faster than the wind. Eventually they arrive in a magic country and dismount. The infatuated poet lies in the lady's lap and she proceeds to show him three 'ferlies', or roads. At this point we need to remember our Bible and the image that it provides of the straight, narrow but difficult path that leads to heaven, and the broad, easy road that leads to hell. These are two of the roads that the Queen of the Fairies shows to Thomas. The third road, however, is the most important one here. It is 'the Road to fair Elfland' along which the poet must be taken. He is to go to a world of wonder that no man has visited before, but, if he speaks one word while he is there, he will not return to his 'ain countrie' for many years.

The poet and the Fairy Queen ride on, wading through rivers whose waters rise to their knees. Neither sun nor moon lights their passage, 'but they heard the roaring of the sea'. The following stanza deepens this sinister impression. The rivers through which they wade are rivers of blood, the blood of all the people who have been slain on earth. Elfland holds terror as well as magic. Eventually the couple reach a garden. The Queen of Fairyland plucks an apple for Thomas and, calling it his wages, tells him 'It will give thee the tongue that can never lee'. Thomas, a man of sterling worth, declares that his tongue is his own and that he is no trickster. He will speak honestly and openly to anybody – and so he has, of course. As the lady had warned him, he will never return to his own country. He is in thrall to the Queen of Elfland for seven years.

John Gilpin – William Cowper

John Gilpin is a comic poem. It has the simple verse forms of the ballads (see pp.114–19), but where those works are serious and often bloody dramas of doom, love and revenge, this poem describes the hilarious escapades of a London merchant. Once again it is most important that we listen to the sound of the words. Where the ballads and poems like *The Rime of the Ancient Mariner* use simple language and subtle rhythms to create their effects, Cowper's poem has a distinctly jog-trot pace. The stressed and unstressed syllables of each line – as well as the obvious rhyme scheme – clatter along in the way that Gilpin's head-strong horse will in the poem itself. The rhythm is designed to amuse us.

The poem begins with a description of Gilpin as a prosperous London linen draper who takes his responsibilities very seriously. He is captain of one of the local military bands. In the second stanza we are told that he has been wedded for twenty years but that he and his wife have never had a holiday. In a sudden moment of extrovert enthusiasm, Mrs Gilpin declares that she and her husband will celebrate their wedding anniversary by driving to 'the Bell at Edmonton/All in a chaise and pair'. She declares that she, her sister, her niece and three children will ride in the chaise itself. Gilpin will have to follow behind on horseback. Gilpin readily agrees to this, saying that his good friend 'the calender' will lend him his horse.

Mrs Gilpin, ever the careful merchant's wife, declares that since the wine at The Bell is rather expensive they will take their own. Gilpin is delighted at her thriftiness. The modesty of the couple is reinforced when the chaise arrives but is parked three doors down the street, so that the neighbours will not think that it is theirs and that they are showing off.

The womenfolk get into the carriage and rattle off through the City of London. Gilpin, meanwhile, tries to mount his friend's horse but immediately falls off it. He is about to remount when he sees three customers coming into his shop. Although it is his wedding anniversary, the thought of making some money so appeals to him that he decides to go and serve them. The customers take a long time to make their minds up about what they want to buy. This is probably just as well for, while they are looking at the goods Gilpin has to offer, his servant Betty comes rushing downstairs declaring that Mrs Gilpin and the other ladies have left the wine behind. He then calls for the thick leather belt from which he usually suspends his sword when he is exercising with his regiment. We will discover the reason for this in a moment. Cowper then tells us how each of the 'two stone bottles' that hold the wine have curving handles. Gilpin threads his belt through the handles, hanging a bottle on each side of him so as to be equally weighted. Then, throwing his long red cloak about him, he sets off on the 'nimble steed' in what he hopes is a cautious manner.

But if Gilpin is a careful man, his horse is of a different metal altogether. Feeling 'a smoother road' beneath him, the horse begins to trot. Gilpin tries to calm him down but his attempts are all in vain. The horse rushes on carrying his helpless rider, and Gilpin can only grasp the mane in both hands and hang on. Since the horse is quite unused to being managed in this way it takes fright and gallops even faster. We must remember that this was an age when wealthy people frequently travelled on horseback. The joke is on Gilpin: he simply does not know how to ride a horse. The animal takes full advantage of this and gallops on faster and faster, causing Gilpin's hat and wig to be swept off his head and his long cloak to fly out behind him like a streamer. At last the button on the cloak gives way and it too is swept off its owner. The two bottles of wine that Gilpin has hung from his broad leather belt are now all too plainly visible.

Meanwhile, the onward career of the horse has attracted quite a crowd. Dogs bark, children scream and people throw up their windows to look out at the amazing sight. They think Gilpin must be riding in a race for a prize of a thousand pounds. So fast is he riding that the turnpike men throw their gates open and let Gilpin pass through in his mad, headlong career. Cowper describes him with his head lying along the horse's neck and then tells us how the bottles of wine 'were shattered at a blow'. The wasted wine runs down the horse's hot flanks which now smoke like meat 'basted' in an oven, while the necks of the broken bottles dangle from Gilpin's belt.

By this time Gilpin has ridden from his home in Cheapside as far as Islington. Eventually he arrives at the 'Wash' at Edmonton, where people publicly launder their clothes. Needless to say, the horse does not stop but rushes through the place, throwing the washing about on all sides. Edmonton is, of course, the place where Gilpin has agreed to join his 'loving wife'. Indeed, she now appears, looking down from the balcony as her husband rushes past. She cries out after him that this is the pub at which they were supposed to meet. She tells him that they are all tired and hungry. Gilpin pathetically cries out 'So am I!' His horse is completely indifferent to his entreaties and actions, however. The beast's only interest is to gallop a further ten miles to Ware and his owner's house. He flies as swiftly as an arrow until he eventually stops at the calender's house, leaving Gilpin quite breathless.

The calender immediately rushes out to ask Gilpin what is the matter. Why has he come without his hat and wig? Why has he come at all? Gilpin humorously tells him that he has come to the calender's house simply because the horse wanted to get there, and adds that his hat and his wig are lying on the road behind him. The calender goes indoors, reappearing with an old hat and wig to replace those that Gilpin has lost. The calender jokingly declares that since his head is twice as big as Gilpin's, the second hat and wig will at least fit him. He then offers Gilpin a wash and something to eat, but Gilpin declares that he must make his way back to his wife at Edmonton, informing his horse that although it has galloped to Ware for its own pleasure, it will now gallop back to Edmonton under his control to make sure that Gilpin fulfils his appointment. 'Ah! luckless speech, and bootless boast!' – although Gilpin now thinks he has the better of the animal, his hopes are all in vain. No sooner has he spoken than the horse hears an ass braying, snorts as loudly as a lion and gallops off. Once more the hapless Gilpin is a victim of his fiery mount. As he is swept away along the road so his second hat and wig are blown from his head. Poor Mrs Gilpin sees her husband racing past in the opposite direction and desperately pulls out 'half-a-crown', telling one of the young serving boys at The Bell that the coin will be his if he brings her husband back safe and well.

The eager youth rides off, catches up with Gilpin and seizes hold of his horse's reins. He only terrifies the animal the more, causing it to gallop even faster. Six gentlemen observe this absurd sight and think that Gilpin must be a thief or highwayman who is being chased by the young servant boy. They raise a tremendous hue and cry and 'join in the pursuit'. Once more, the amazed officers at the turnpike open their gates and let the racing Gilpin through. Eventually he arrives at the town before the young man and only dismounts from his horse when he is back at his own house. Hoping for a quiet celebration of his twentieth wedding anniversary with his wife, Gilpin has been swept all the way across London and back again. Cowper finishes the poem by declaring that if such an adventure should happen to Gilpin again, he hopes to be there to see it.

Peter Grimes – George Crabbe

Peter Grimes is a moral tale. It shows the evil that men do when they refuse a Christian view of the world and how they are horribly punished for their sins. Crabbe has used a somewhat rigid verse form for the poem (see pp. 114–19). You will notice that each line has ten syllables and that the whole is written in couplets. As you read through the work, however, you should notice two further things: first, the power and energy with which Crabbe packs his verse, and, secondly, the feelings of horror and pity he makes us feel for his evil hero.

The work opens with a description of the life of the hero's father, 'Old Peter Grimes'. He is a God-fearing man who works hard and lives peacefully and contentedly with his wife and son. He is described as a 'quiet' man who comes to town to sell his fish. He is polite to the people he meets and in turn is loved by them. On Sundays he takes a rest from his trade and teaches his young son Peter how to pray. However, for all the father's virtuous concern, 'the stubborn boy from care broke loose'. Crabbe clearly wishes to present young Peter as an adolescent rebel. He refuses to pray with his father and, when his father begs him, the boy abuses him. He scorns the old man's care and we will see that it is this behaviour that helps drive Old Peter to an early grave.

Notice how quickly Crabbe telescopes events here. No sooner do we learn that young Peter is a rebellious child, than we see him as a drunken young man weeping with remorse at his father's death. Only when he is drunk does young Peter feel ashamed of his behaviour. He recalls how he reviled the old man, refused to behave as a dutiful child and rejected all attempts to make him read the Bible. Old Peter Grimes is shown telling his son that the Bible is 'the word of life'. Young Peter's reply is that the loose living he enjoys 'is the life itself'. The old man is horrified by such impiety. Peter continues to abuse him, calling him a tyrant when his father tries to check his behaviour, and even hitting him so hard that he falls to the ground fatally hurt. Crabbe describes the blow as 'sacrilegious'. It is a sin. As the groaning father speaks his last words, so we see that it is the blow that has finally killed him and we come to realize that this is the first of the murders that the hero of the poem commits.

Having presented us with these images of rebellious behaviour, guilt and sin – feelings that will be of the greatest importance to the rest of the work – Crabbe then writes a short paragraph which describes the pathetic, drink-sodden state into which Peter Grimes has already fallen:

> On an inn-settle, in his maudlin grief,
> This he revolved, and drank for his relief.

What a powerful picture of moral squalor this couplet provides.

Crabbe next shows us the young Peter Grimes, free at last from parental restraint, but bitter at the fact that he has to earn his living and cannot spend all his time drinking and playing cards. But Grimes is not merely lazy and pathetically self-indulgent – not simply a weak character – he is also an evil man. He looks greedily at other people's possessions. He does not care for law or justice. Instead, he becomes a thief. When he has finished fishing the sea, he goes and robs on land. He steals fruit and animals from nearby farms. As the sins he commits accumulate, so he gets ever further removed from an easy, loving relationship with mankind. His guilt and shame isolate him. He is alone in his squalor. Crabbe vividly suggests the wretchedness of his life through the description of the hovel in which Grimes lives. Here, in his lonely den, surrounded by the things that he has stolen, Grimes becomes ever more isolated and ever more sinful. Crabbe tells us that he now has a 'cruel soul'. He feels the need to be yet more wicked, yet more vengeful on that world around him which his sins have forced him to hate. He needs someone whom he can dominate completely and brutalize; somebody to punish and abuse. In his imagination he pictures 'some obedient boy' who will serve this function.

Crabbe then tells us that Grimes has heard about the workhouses in London. If you have read *Oliver Twist*, you will perhaps remember how cruel such places were. The children who lived in them were often appallingly treated and starved of food, affection and hope. The people who ran these evil places were often themselves poor and corrupt. Grimes has heard that for 'a trifling sum' of money they will sell off the orphaned boys in their care, happy to make them 'toiling slaves' for the sake of a few wretched pence.

Lines 59–64 provide a most depressing picture in which life is cheap and those who cannot protect themselves are the helpless victims of men who exploit them. When he has thought about all this for some time, Grimes decides to act. He finds a boy, buys him and so acquires a 'slave'. The second of the brutally horrific episodes in the poem is about to begin.

You will remember that Grimes's hovel is placed in dreary isolation: he is thus isolated both physically as well as by his evil, ambitious nature. Away in his hovel he can do what he likes without the other townsfolk being too obviously aware of what is going on. And, for a while, they are not particularly interested. A few of them see the newly acquired 'slave' being driven in Peter's trap, but they do not ask about Peter's beating him with a rope or why the boy is stooping under the pain and bruising that Grimes has inflicted on him. They cannot actually see the weals, nor do they observe the lad 'shiv'ring in the winter's cold'. For the moment these people are uncaring. They do not ask why Peter fails to feed the lad properly. They do not urge charity. They do not explain to Grimes that if he looks after the boy properly then he will work better for him. Indeed, at this point in the poem, the inhabitants of the town are criticized for their lack of imaginative sympathy. When they hear Grimes beating the boy they merely comment in a callous way: 'Grimes is at his exercise'. A picture of an uncaring, squalid and unimaginative little world is brought vividly before our eyes.

It is for Crabbe to rouse our feelings of pity as well as contempt. If we despise Grimes and the townsfolk, we are also made to feel very sorry for the boy. The sympathy which Grimes and the townsfolk lack is forced on us by the power of Crabbe's language. Look at the lines 79–88. What power Crabbe packs into the rhythm here! Consider the first line of this section: 'Pinn'd, beaten, cold, pinch'd, threaten'd, and abused –'. The stressed syllables of each of these ugly words fall with the monotonous, cruel rhythm of the rope with which Peter beats the boy. The lad lives in a world of suffering from which there seems to be no escape. When he tries to work he is punished and starved. His life is wretched while he is awake and yet he is allowed almost no time in which to sleep. The elegance of line 82 – 'Struck if he wept, and yet compell'd to weep' – is in horrible contrast to the brutality it describes. The poor child cannot ever be free from suffering and tears. Even when he tries to pray he is beaten, while the pathological cruelty of Grimes is shown as Crabbe describes how he 'grinn'd in horrid glee'. At last this evil creature has found his perfect victim. He torments the boy for 'three sad years' after which the lad dies. Again, you should note how vividly lines 89–92 describe the child's pathetic existence.

The all but indifferent townsfolk at last begin to ask questions when they discover that the boy is dead. Grimes growls out his lying answer. He tells them that he found the boy 'lifeless in his bed'. The suggestion is that the child had died a natural death. Grimes even tries to make this sound convincing by calling the boy 'Poor Sam'. This is the first and only time that we hear the lad's name. Up to this moment he has been a nameless, suffering waif. Nonetheless, for all Grimes's hypocritical attempts to cover up what has happened, the townsfolk begin to doubt the truth of the stories they have heard. They begin to wonder about how the boy was fed, how often he was punished, how hard he had to work. They have become suspicious. But since they can prove nothing, Grimes appears to have got away with his second crime.

Grimes's thirst for cruelty has not yet been slaked. 'Another boy with equal ease was found'. Grimes claims that this lad dies when he falls from the mast into the hold of the fishing vessel where the live catch is stored. Notice how savage and effective Crabbe's irony is here. He described the suffering of the first boy in some detail. However, when he comes to describe the fate of the second child, he provides almost no details of his life at all. The reader is left to fill these in himself. We sense that the second boy has been made to suffer just as much as the first. We also see that Grimes's lies are becoming less and less convincing. Though he has claimed that the second boy's death was an accident, the townsfolk do not really believe him. It is extremely unlikely that a boy falling from a mast on to a soft bed of live fish in the hold would actually be killed. He might be badly hurt, but it is improbable that he would actually die. 'So reason'd men.' Grimes tries to back up his lies. He declares that he is telling the truth, that the boy was an idler who played all day long. However, this time the matter has come to court. Clearly the townsfolk are deeply suspicious of Grimes, even if they can still prove nothing. They demand that a jury inquire into the matter. Nonetheless, Grimes is such a brazen liar that he gets away with his

26 *Passnotes:* **Narrative Poems**

undoubted third murder. He receives nothing but a warning and is told to close the hatchway over the hold in future when his boys are climbing the mast. Even Grimes's conscience is moved by this, but, since he has got away with a third murder, he remains confident. He returns to the 'slave-shop' and obtains another boy.

Though we have undoubtedly felt sorry for the two boys who have already fallen victim to Grimes's savage nature, the mere physical appearance of the third lad makes us instantly feel even more pity for him. We are told that he has 'manners soft and mild'. Even the poorest of the townsfolk feel that he must be of noble birth. Perhaps he is the illegitimate son of some aristocrat who has seduced a 'humble maid'. They realize that he is 'a gracious lad'. His patience, sadness and air of refinement make his suffering appear all the more dreadful. At last the sympathy of the townsfolk is roused. They begin seriously to look after him. They provide him with 'fire, food, and comfort'.

The following paragraph (lines 138–52) describes the horrible death of the third 'slave'. We are told that Grimes has made an exceptional catch of fish and has decided to sell it in London. He takes the sickly boy with him. At first they sail safely down the river and the boy contains his fears until they reach the open, 'angry sea'. Now the lad is truly terrified and clings to Grimes's knees. The boat grows leaky. The wind blows ever more strongly. The little boat is tossed up and down for a long time, long enough indeed for Grimes to run out of drink. He grows furious at this. He turns on his apprentice and 'the rest we must suppose'. In other words, in his furious drunkenness on the storm-tossed and leaky little boat he kills the boy. Clearly he dumps the body overboard. Grimes himself returns safely to the town and claims that he tried to make for harbour but first 'the fish, and then th'apprentice died'.

This time no one believes him. The pity and indignation of the poor fisherwomen have been roused and they openly accuse Grimes of drowning his apprentice. Grimes is summoned before the 'burghers' to explain what has happened. Once more Grimes tries to brazen the matter out. He claims that he cared for the boy, but the mayor declares sternly that although he is going to let Grimes go free – he cannot actually prove that Grimes murdered the lad – he forbids him ever to have a boy servant again. He adds that should Grimes appear before the court again, then he will be severely punished.

Grimes now lives in a deeper isolation than he has known before.

He is hated: he has no one to help him, he rows alone, he casts his nets alone. 'He toil'd and rail'd; he groan'd and swore alone.'

Crabbe now begins to induce in the reader flickers of sympathy for this evil man in his intense isolation. He does this partly by describing the dull and dreary landscape in which this pathetic murderer is obliged to work. Each day he sees 'the same dull views'. The landscape is marshy, the flat horizon is broken only by 'a blighted tree'. When the tide is high there is only an empty vista of water to stare over; when the tide runs low, there is only dank mud to be seen, dreary stakes driven into the sides of the banks, heaps of weed and the 'sun-burnt tar' on Grimes's little boat. This whole paragraph (lines 170-80) creates a wonderfully melancholy picture. You may like to compare the way in which this dreary landscape reflects the equally dreary soul of Grimes with the way in which the seascapes in *The Ancient Mariner* tell us what the hero of that poem is enduring.

It is amidst so much melancholy and lonely toil that Grimes hides himself from mankind (line 185). Alone with his guilt and suffering, he watches the lazy water 'in its hot slimy channel slowly glide'. His mood is 'dull and hopeless'. His only companions are the eels, the 'gaping mussels', the 'tuneless cry' of the gulls, and the call of the bitterns. Here indeed is a desolate landscape that produces desolate feelings. Everything that Grimes sees or hears oppresses his 'soul with misery, grief and fear'. This passage of landscape description is one of the finest achievements in the whole poem. Just as Keats, in *The Eve of St Agnes*, can describe rich and beautiful things in ways that excite our imagination, so in *Peter Grimes*, when Crabbe describes the bleak landscape of Suffolk, he makes us feel the despair of his hero. Slowly we begin to feel a little pity for this evil and lonely man skulking in the marshes.

Crabbe also tells us of three places Grimes is frightened to go. He has to pass them in the course of his work, but each time he does so he is so afraid that he whistles to keep his spirits up. We begin to guess why these places are so awful to him – clearly they are connected with the murder of the three boys – but only later on in the poem do we actually learn why Grimes is so terrified of them. For the moment, Crabbe plants a suspicion in our minds and lets it grow while he tells us of other matters.

He tells us how Grimes cannot escape from his suffering, how he is shunned by the men in the town and berated by the women. Even the children point him out as 'the wicked man'. He grunts and curses at the people around him and wants only to be alone. But when he is alone, 'the same dull scenes' that he is forced to look at become even more oppressive. He goes on grimly working, but Crabbe tells us that even the seagulls are better fishermen than he. Grimes begins to sink. Though he has been a physically sturdy man, his body is now racked with 'cold nervous tremblings'. Nightmares frighten him; he sees horrible visions that would 'amaze' even the most intelligent and level-headed man. The horrors are diabolic (line 228). Grimes begins to hate the way in which he is forced to live apart from other people. Nonetheless, when others do come near him he starts away in terror.

Crabbe tells us how, during the summertime, holiday-makers come to the area and look across the bay with their 'glasses'. Stories begin to circulate about a lonely fisherman who, using neither net or hook, drifts around the 'gliding waves'. He seems to stare out lazily at everything around him. He is 'bewilder'd'. He seems to be in the grip of some supernatural power, to be cursed or meditating on sin. Of course, the figure being observed is the wretched Grimes.

People begin to take a greater interest in him. They ask why he does not repent of what he has done. Grimes merely trembles, leaves his boat and, with increasing anguish, grows hysterical and runs about the countryside. Eventually, no longer able to look after himself, he is placed in the care of the parish. His guilt has driven him mad and this suffering and isolated man is obliged to be looked after by other people.

The poet describes him as 'a lost, lone man, so harass'd and undone' that the women of the town begin to feel sorry for him, even though they cannot altogether forget the 'crimes' he has committed. Finally a priest is brought. The true horror of Grimes's guilt is about to be revealed. The townsfolk watch him shaking, noisily grinding his teeth, glaring out in his fit, swearing and clenching his fist. As the priest listens to the desperate cries of the dying Grimes, so he begins to piece together the fragmentary evidence of the man's guilt. Grimes grows calmer as he gets weaker. The townsfolk watch 'the cold death-drop glaze his sunken eyes'. But Grimes is not yet dead. With a final effort he begins to speak, but it is as if he is speaking to some ghost or phantom beside him rather than to real people. Indeed, he does not recognize the townsfolk gathered around him. Crabbe tells us that what he says is 'part confession and the rest defence'. It is 'a madman's tale' in which Grimes partly reveals what he has done and suffered and partly disguises the truth.

He begins to describe how he has seen the ghost of his father – the first person he murdered. He still hates the old man but now he has a new reason for doing so. At first it is not easy to guess this reason. Grimes mumbles about how the old man places 'them' before Grimes's vision. What are these things, we may ask. We may guess, but, for the moment, we are not directly told. What we do know is that the visions Grimes has seen have driven him mad. Perhaps they are connected with the three places that fill him with so much fear.

Grimes goes on to describe how, one hot silent afternoon, he went fishing. He caught nothing. He believes that the malignant ghost of his father is responsible for this and curses his father for torturing him in this way. He then declares how he sat looking on the running stream. An apparition appeared to him. It was like a dream but it was not a dream at all. He then sees other spirits rise out of the water in front of him. One of these spirits is his father who holds, in either hand, 'a thin pale boy'. They glide in a ghastly manner over the water. Grimes wants to strike out at them but they smile at the oar with which he threatens them and disappear back below the water. Every day Grimes goes out he sees the same horrific sight. It chastens him. He prays that the ghostly figures will disappear. They take no notice of him. The boat stays stockstill. The ghosts urge Grimes to commit suicide. Every day they repeat the same message. Grimes says 'to hear and mark them daily was my doom'. He desperately tries to row away from them, but he fails and is forced to listen to their sad, insistent wailing. Grimes declares that his father should have pity on him. The ghost merely freezes him with his look. A hollow groan rises through the water each time Grimes strikes out at the figures. He is bitterly resentful of the fact that they have no compassion for him.

It is, of course, precisely in the three places Grimes is most afraid to go that the three ghosts appear to him. He is obliged to stare at them for hours. They try repeatedly to tempt him into suicide. The ghosts of the boys particularly enjoy Grimes's suffering. The punishment that he is suffering is truly horrific. We may well think Grimes deserves it, but our horror and our pity are also moved by the remorseless way in which the ghosts keep reappearing.

We are told of the ghosts' final appearance, how, on 'one fierce summer-day' they emerged and glared at Grimes. While he is fainting, the old man scoops up the sea-water in his hand. Flame and blood begin to dance around his ghostly form. He tells Grimes to look closely and then he throws 'the hot-red liquor' in his face. Grimes is almost driven mad by the pain and roars in agony. Nonetheless, the ghosts will not go away and Grimes himself cannot escape. They force him to look even more carefully at the flame and blood. Eventually, Grimes sees hell itself, horrors that he cannot even begin to describe. He hears the shrieks of the guilty spirits. They tell him that the suffering they undergo day in, day out, is everlasting. It is a more intense and dreadful version of the suffering Grimes has endured in the bleak landscape where he works.

As Grimes describes this awful vision, so he comes to a sudden halt and gazes out hysterically at the people around his bed. He tries to speak again but fails. Death comes fast upon him but, as he dies, he croaks, 'again they come!' His last waking second offers a glimpse of the infernal punishment to which he is condemned for ever more.

Michael – William Wordsworth

Wordsworth describes *Michael* as a 'pastoral' poem. This means that it is set in the countryside and concerns country people. For Wordsworth such a life was one of profound significance and beauty. He believed that living close to nature made people honest and deeply content. In the joy and beauty that surrounded them they could learn to appreciate all that was truly holy about life. One of the things that Wordsworth is concerned about investigating in *Michael* is the effect on a young man of being removed from this world. For Wordsworth the results were truly tragic. The young man in his poem – his name is Luke – leaves the beautiful landscape in which he had been brought up. He goes to the city and, although he lives a virtuous life for a while, is quickly corrupted:

> ... Meantime Luke began
> To slacken in his duty: and, at length,
> He in the dissolute city gave himself
> To evil courses: ignominy and shame
> Fell on him, so that he was driven at last
> To seek a hiding-place beyond the seas.

The poem is a tragedy about the destruction of a young man's moral and physical well-being and of the anguish this inflicts on his parents, particularly his father, Michael.

The poem opens with a description of a rugged landscape that soon opens into 'a hidden valley' of great beauty. It is an isolated place and beside the brook that runs through it 'appears a heap of unhewn stones'. These stones are one of the very few signs of human life that the poet shows us at the opening of the work and, of course, they will have great significance as the only visible record of the tragedy that Wordsworth is to relate. He declares that his will be a simple, wholesome story. He also tells us some important things about himself. He tells us how powerfully nature worked on him when he was a boy, that he was not a scholarly child but 'careless of books'. This means that he took little interest in them. He received far more powerful lessons from the beauty of the landscape about him and he felt deeply at one with its beauty. It inspired him. By surrendering himself to the excitement and wonder of nature, he learnt far more about 'man, the heart of man, and human life' than he could ever have learned from reading. It is something of this deep insight into the power of nature over people that Wordsworth wishes to show us in *Michael*.

The paragraph beginning at line 40 describes the old shepherd's active and virtuous life. He is a fit, morally upright man concerned with the well-being of those around him. In line 61 we learn that he is over eighty but still vigorous. By the end of the paragraph we have learned that the beauty of the countryside in which he lives and the healthy, physical exertions it forces upon him have a 'strong hold on his affections'. His whole virtuous being is at one with the landscape around him. Just as Wordsworth himself had learned to love man by being at one with nature, so it is with the old shepherd. A country life has made him virtuous.

In the succeeding paragraph we are given glimpses of Michael's happy home life. We see his wife who is, like him, virtuous and hard-working. Her life is given over to making a home for Michael, their son and the two sheep dogs. The whole family are known for their diligence. Wordsworth praises their 'endless industry', their complete lack of idleness and self-indulgence. Their existence, like the food they eat, is simple and wholesome. Their constant hard work is a further aspect of this frugal honesty and they are loved far and wide for their virtuous life. The lamp that gleams out from their cottage at night is a symbol of their happy and contented existence. To all those around them, the shining lamp is a constant comfort. People christen the cottage 'The Evening Star'.

Though Michael is evidently fond of his wife, the paragraph beginning with line 140 makes it clear that his deepest affections are for his son. As Luke grows strong and healthy, so the old man sees his own life being relived by the boy. His fondness for him as a baby is made clear at the end of the paragraph. Yet, if Michael adores his son, he is far from a sentimental and indulgent father. We would not expect him to be so. He shows his love for his son by helping him to grow up in a disciplined and secure environment. Notice how Wordsworth rapidly describes Luke's progress from babyhood through to boyhood. When Luke is a mere ten-year-old he is already strong enough to walk through the countryside all day with his father. We then come to the time when Luke is eighteen. Everything seems ideal: secure, upright, moral, stern yet loving. However, disaster nonetheless falls on the family.

Though not a wealthy man, Michael has made himself reasonably comfortable and prosperous through sheer, determined hard work. Indeed, as we are told in lines 375-6, only by the time he is forty does he own his entire farm. He is proud but not vain of his possessions. As we have seen, he is deeply attached to the landscape in which he works. Suddenly it is placed in jeopardy.

Michael has guaranteed a loan taken out by his nephew. If the nephew loses the money and cannot pay it back, Michael will be forced to cover the debt. He will have to pay for his nephew's failings. He is now summoned to do just this. In one fell stroke he has lost half his possessions, the very possessions that he has worked so hard to secure over the past forty years. The blow devastates him and he turns to his wife for comfort. (We learn, for the first time, that her name is Isabel.) All Michael can do at the moment is to express his intense sorrow. His whole being is attached to the landscape in which he works and which he has laboured so hard to own. The idea that it may have to be sold and 'pass into a stranger's hand' is unbearable to him. He suggests that the grief might kill him and that he could never lie quietly in his grave. He forgives the nephew who has caused him this anguish but, for the moment, the old shepherd sees no hope. The claims that money makes have destroyed all the well-being that a healthy country life can nurture in the heart and soul of a man. Something of deep, spiritual goodness has been threatened and it seems as if it is to be destroyed. Michael resolves to do all in his power to prevent this. He is not simply saving his money and possessions; he is saving the beautiful world around him – the natural world – that has lent so much meaning to his life.

At last he thinks of a possible solution. He tells us of a 'kinsman', a relation, who is a prosperous businessman. He believes that if only he can send Luke to this man as an apprentice then the boy will quickly earn enough money to pay off the debt and thus save the farm. Though Michael will have to part from his beloved son for some time, at least there will be hope. It is a hope with which his wife also comforts herself.

She remembers the story of a poor child in the village who was kitted up with a few humble things to sell, made his way to London and eventually to a fortune. This young man clearly had strength and a spirit of enterprise. At the end of his successful life he left his money to the poor and built a beautiful chapel in his village. Such thoughts comfort Isabel. Perhaps her own son will pursue the same course. Perhaps he too will be a virtuous apprentice.

A certain air of happiness comes upon the distressed household as the old couple think about this solution to their problems. Nonetheless, the reality of their sacrifice slowly dawns on them. Though Isabel dutifully sets about making clothes for Luke, she realizes that Michael is deeply distressed by the thought of being parted from his son. She realizes that he is 'troubled in his sleep'. She even begs her son not to go, telling him that his father will die if he leaves him. Luke calms her fears. A letter then arrives from the kinsman declaring that he would be only too happy to help out and to employ Luke. The letter fills the couple with joy. Wordsworth touchingly describes how they read it 'ten times or more', and then showed it to all their neighbours. Michael declares that his son will leave the following day. Although his wife tries to protest, she has at length to give her consent.

We have seen that Michael has brought up his son in a disciplined, unsentimental way and that he loves him dearly. Now, as the moment of parting nears, so the old man's deep affection for his son shows in the tears in his eyes. He tells Luke how he has looked after him since the day that he was born 'with increasing love'. As they walk out into the beautiful countryside around them, the old man's emotions are deeply stirred. He reflects upon the healthy and happy life they have led so far. We see how nature has deepened their feelings. The old man tells his son how he loves those who helped him in his childhood. He describes how he has toiled hard to be the master of the beautiful landscape around him. He wants nothing more than that his own son should inherit the beauty and spiritual strength he himself has known. Nonetheless, he realizes that for the sake of money the boy must leave him.

In the next paragraph the old man talks with an almost breaking heart. He describes how, despite his eighty-four years, he is still strong and will labour on his own, doing all the work which he had hoped Luke would help him with. He talks emotionally 'of the links of love'

Michael – William Wordsworth

that have bound father and son together. He knows that love such as this, stern but deeply affectionate and nurtured amid a beautiful landscape, is the most powerful and moral feeling that a man may have. He also guesses that a life away from such sustaining affection is potentially dangerous. He is worried about what may happen to Luke. In the city Luke may well meet 'evil men'.

In his wise and simple way Michael knows that only his son's memories of his secure and loving childhood will save him from temptation. He needs desperately to concentrate Luke's thoughts on all the goodness that has surrounded him. He begs the boy to lay the first stone of the new sheepcote that he is building. It is a symbolic gesture. It means that although Luke is going to be away he is still a part of the life of his father's farm. If only the boy will turn his mind to this scene whenever he is tempted by the life of the wicked city, he will be redeemed by memories of the love and decent way of life that he has known. But this deep and moving gesture fails. The old man's passionate monologue ends with the mention of his own death. We know from the start of the poem that the sheepcote is never built; it remains 'a straggling heap of unhewn stones'. The father will die, the boy will be corrupted. He will not remember the goodness and the virtue of his upbringing.

Father and son have parted tearfully, but at first things go well. The kinsman who has apprenticed Luke writes to his parents to tell them that he is prospering, while the boy himself writes 'loving letters, full of wondrous news'. His parents are delighted. Such happiness even gives the old man the strength and confidence to try and build a little more of the sheepfold. But it is a futile gesture. The memories of Luke's boyhood are not enough to save him from 'the dissolute city'. So powerful are the temptations around him – and so quickly do they operate – that memories of his virtuous father and the sheepfold that they began to build together cannot save him. Luke grows lazy and dishonest and eventually has to 'seek a hiding-place beyond the seas'. You may remember at this point how Luke's mother recalled the boy sent out of the village who made himself a fortune in foreign lands. We described him as the virtuous apprentice. How very different Luke's life is. He goes abroad not to make money and so save his parents' farm but to flee from justice. He is the idle apprentice whose life ends in ignominy and shame.

The penultimate paragraph of the poem is a moving one. It shows how Michael still treasures the memory of his son for all that the boy has lived a dissolute life. Though the boy has forgotten him, destroyed his hopes and failed to provide the money that will save the farm, his father still recalls him with the deepest affection as he struggles with his hard life amid the rugged landscape. From time to time he sits by the sheepfold that he and Luke had started to build. Though the boy has long forgotten the work and all it stood for, for Michael the sheepfold is a symbol of the son he has lost but whom he still loves. For the last seven years of his life Michael goes frequently to the pile of stones but eventually old age and sorrow wear him down. He leaves 'the work unfinished' when he dies. His wife survives him by only three years and after her death what she and her husband have most feared inevitably happens: the farm is sold and passes 'into a stranger's hand'. The new owner pulls their cottage down and ploughs up the land upon which it stood. 'Great changes' have taken place: barely a fragment of these virtuous but blighted lives remain. Indeed, only an oak tree and the unfinished sheepfold survive as testimonies to the past life. The unfinished sheepfold is no longer a symbol to Luke of the virtue and happiness that he knew as a child; rather, it stands as a sad memorial of deeply loved and beautiful lives which were ruined.

The Rime of the Ancient Mariner – Samuel Taylor Coleridge

The Rime of the Ancient Mariner is one of the central masterpieces of English literature, a haunting poem by a haunted man who, only near the close of his narrative, informs us that he has a hypnotic and supernatural hold over us:

> I pass, like night, from land to land;
> I have strange power of speech;
> That moment that his face I see,
> I know the man that must hear me:
> To him my tale I teach.

Just as the Wedding-Guest at the start of the poem is held spellbound by the Ancient Mariner 'with his glittering eye', so we the readers are held equally in thrall.

At the start of the poem the Ancient Mariner waylays one of three guests who have been invited to a wedding. He obtrudes his strange and fearsome presence on a young man about to go to a happy, social celebration. The guest wonders why he has been stopped in this way, but, again, it is only at the close of the poem that he is told by the Ancient Mariner himself that he is one of the people for whom the Mariner's story will have a powerful, emotional significance. At the start of the poem the Wedding-Guest is happy and carefree. At the close, when he has heard the whole of the Mariner's story, he will be 'a sadder and a wiser man'.

At first he protests against being stopped. The wedding-feast is about to take place and the youth tells us that he is 'next of kin' to the bridegroom. All the other guests have assembled, the feast has been prepared and the musicians are cheerfully playing their music. The Mariner takes no notice whatsoever of the Wedding-Guest's objections. He grasps him with 'his skinny hand' and forces him to hear his tale. There will be no joyful celebrations for the Wedding-Guest to enjoy;

rather, like the Ancient Mariner himself, he will be torn from a pleasant, social gathering and be obliged to hear a story of overwhelming isolation, loneliness and spiritual torment.

Notice how brilliantly Coleridge contrasts these themes. On the one hand we are presented with the awesome and isolated figure of the Ancient Mariner himself while, on the other, the Wedding-Guest makes us imagine the wedding celebrations themselves. Why has Coleridge chosen a wedding to begin his poem? Surely because a wedding is the happiest of celebrations, a festivity conducted around love, hope and, above all, a sense of community. It is precisely a divorce from such an easy and loving social world that the Mariner will force the Wedding-Guest to participate in. His tale will not be a simple one of joy and revelry, of normal people and normal happiness. It will be the very opposite: a terrifying, wonderful story not of this world, a story about a man who knows dreadful things. By forcing the Wedding-Guest to listen to him rather than go to the feast, the Ancient Mariner begins to inflict upon the young man something of his own sense of isolation. The Wedding-Guest is placed under the Mariner's spell, and soon, as the old man's story begins to unfold its mysterious charms, so he is involved in experiences very different to those which he had expected to enjoy.

As the Mariner stretches out his skinny hand, we begin to sense the power being asserted over the young man. His immediate reaction is understandable. He protests. He demands that the Ancient Mariner let him go and he threatens to beat him with his staff. But notice how the Mariner exerts his hypnotic power. He is not in the least moved by the young man's protests nor afraid of being beaten by him. 'He holds him with his glittering eye.' A stare is sufficient to disarm him and make him as meek as a 'three year's child'. Not through physical violence does the Ancient Mariner exert his hypnotic influence: he disarms the Wedding-Guest with a single penetrating glance. Clearly there is something demonic about the power of this man. Through some strange inward force 'the Mariner hath his will'. The Wedding-Guest quietly sits down on a stone beside him, no longer master of his actions. Now that he has subdued him in this way, the Ancient Mariner can begin to weave his spellbinding narrative.

Part of the tremendous force of *The Rime of the Ancient Mariner* lies in the way in which Coleridge manages to create very strong contrasts,

The Rime of the Ancient Mariner – Samuel Taylor Coleridge

as here between the happy atmosphere of the wedding-feast and the awesome appearance of the isolated old man himself. Now, as the Mariner begins to tell his story of loneliness and spiritual death, so he begins his tale not with doom-laden fear but in a cheerful, happy manner. His description of the ship sailing out of the harbour creates a joyful feeling of expectancy within us. It is a feeling that will be undermined in a way that we can hardly imagine. Only much later, after a tremendous and terrible voyage, will the significance of the lighthouse and the 'kirk' beside the harbour take on a new meaning (see pp. 53–5). In the next two stanzas (lines 29–34) the Mariner continues his description of the ease and happiness of the early days of the voyage. However, these feelings have already been questioned.

Delightful though the description of the voyage is, the Wedding-Guest hears, as he listens to the Mariner, the sounds of revelry coming from the wedding hall. The 'loud bassoon' is playing. The beautiful bride 'hath pac'd into the hall'. Her simple loveliness is compared to a rose, and around this image of love and fulfilment cluster the musicians themselves, loudly playing their instruments in celebration of the forthcoming marriage. The young man beats his breast. He longs to be in the hall with his rejoicing friends, but he cannot be. As he sits under the spell of the Mariner's words, with the sounds of revelry in the background, so he begins to experience some of the old man's own isolation and unhappiness.

And now even the mood of the voyage alters. At first an exciting adventure, it now changes to something awe-inspiringly beautiful. A storm begins to rage. For weeks this storm drives the little boat through the frozen marvels of an Antarctic sea. Notice the tremendous vividness with which Coleridge brings this strange landscape before us. Vast icebergs as high as the boat itself and glimmering with the rich and magical greenness of emeralds float across the storm-tossed ocean. Snowy cliffs surround the little boat and, as the Mariner and the rest of his crew stare out from the 'dismal' wastes around them, so the awful isolation begins to frighten them. They can see no sign of life at all, no shape of men or beasts; nor is there any sound of living beings to be heard, only the nightmarish noise of ice cracking, growling and howling about them. They have sailed into a world that is at once natural and supernatural, beautiful and awe-inspiring, but also profoundly lonely and deeply threatening.

Let us think a little more carefully about these landscapes. If we are only reading the poem for the adventure that it provides then, there is adventure and drama here in abundance. What could be more dramatic than a little boat isolated in an Antarctic sea, cut off from the life around it and threatened on all sides by forces beyond man's control? Yet, as we read on, so we will see that the poem is far more than a simple adventure. The landscapes are not merely wonders of nature, things for man to pit his physical strength against. If we listen to the poetry and let the hypnotic magic of the Mariner's words work on our deeper feelings, then we will begin to see that these descriptions of landscapes can have a much deeper effect on us. They are not the simple thrills and wonders of a cartoon strip but something much more significant. They are accurate pictures of the world surrounding the little boat, but they are also mental landscapes. The vast tracts of empty, snowy space, the absence of any other creature, begin to impose an awful sense of isolation on us. Here is a world where each man seems to be obliged to confront loneliness and fear. What the Mariner sees about him is an outward and physical sign of the appalling loneliness, fear and isolation that he will later experience in his own heart.

To appreciate the full richness of *The Rime of the Ancient Mariner* it is essential that we let the magic of the words work on our deepest feelings. We must put ourselves in the same position as the young Wedding-Guest and feel ourselves caught by the demonic power of the old man. We must allow ourselves to be held by his 'glittering eye' and restrained by his 'skinny hand'. We must let the real world about us recede as we listen, for we too are the select audience on whom the Mariner's tale will have a profoundly disturbing effect. We, too, as we are drawn into the power and mystery of what the old man has to say, will be affected and changed by it. If we are prepared to lend our hearts and ears to the Ancient Mariner's words, the deeper concerns of Coleridge's poem will work on us as they do on the Wedding-Guest. We too may well be 'sadder and wiser' for the experience of attending to the poem.

The picture of isolation and loneliness, of physical strength and emotional panic that the Mariner's description of the Antarctic sea has created for us is evidently a very powerful one. Then, once more, Coleridge creates a strong contrast. Across the frozen horrors on which the Ancient Mariner and his crew are being tortured flies an albatross.

It is the first living thing that any of them have seen for a long time. They welcome the bird with cries of affection and call out to it with blessings and gratitude in their hearts. To men isolated in the vulnerable little boat, the appearance of the albatross is as welcome as a meeting with 'a Christian soul'. Their sense of relief and pleasure at seeing a living creature is perfectly understandable, but it will help us to appreciate the particular significance of the albatross if we realize that this gawky, ugly bird is part of sailors' folklore. An albatross is a bird of good omen and its appearance around the masts of boats is supposed to bring good luck and good weather.

In the ghastly conditions of the Antarctic, the sudden appearance of this bird is thus doubly welcome. But again we should stop to question our emotions a little more deeply. So closely have we identified with the feelings of fear that the Ancient Mariner and his crew have felt, that we should pause to wonder if the relief caused by the appearance of the bird has a function similar to the feelings aroused by the landscape. We have seen that landscape was both a real world about the ship and also a symbolic place, an expression of an inward isolation and fear. It is just the same with the bird. The feeling of love for another creature that springs spontaneously in the heart of all the sailors is an emotion of supreme significance in the poem. It is, quite simply, an expression of love for the living world. The albatross is not merely a good luck charm, an object of superstitious folklore. The feeling of sheer joy that it rouses in the sailors' hearts as it flies above the boat is an almost sacred emotion of joyous unity with the living world that is the source of all goodness. At the very heart of *The Rime of the Ancient Mariner* lies a profound intuition of truth. Only through a spontaneous and unquestioning love of the living world about us – men and women, animals and all created things – can man be most truly happy and most truly human. The Mariner learns this only by cutting himself off from the natural world and suffering a living hell of isolation.

The way in which the joy of the Mariner's crew at the arrival of the bird is expressed is both natural and touching. As the bird flies closer to them, circling around the mast, they offer it things to eat. Because of their joy and love, the charm of the albatross works its magic. The ice around the boat splits and she sails on safely. A wind now springs up, the boat rolls happily and the playful albatross comes to the sailors whenever they call it. It comes particularly at the time of evening prayers. We shall see later how this sense of happy and loving community, bound together by a religious faith, is of great significance to the poem as a whole (see p. 63).

The Wedding-Guest has clearly been moved as strongly as we have by the Mariner's words, and he looks with puzzlement at the old man's troubled face. He can only assume that the Ancient Mariner is plagued by fiends. Why should he be? Why should a man who has been so blessed, who has known such happiness and release from danger, appear so troubled? The old man gives his reason with great simplicity:

> – With my cross-bow
> I shot the Albatross.

No explanation for his action is ever given. But if we read the poem particularly carefully, with an ear to all its nuances, we well understand exactly what has happened. The Mariner has committed a terrible sin. He has destroyed more than a life: he has in one simple savage action destroyed the love and joy that came to the sailors in their torment. He has also destroyed their luck. For all this he must suffer. The action needs no explanation. We sense how awful it is, how sinfully destructive. For the moment that is enough.

The Ancient Mariner begins to pay for his crime almost immediately. The sun rises out of the sea hidden in mist and, although a 'good south wind' continues to carry the boat along, an even greater sense of isolation is felt now that the albatross is dead. This theme of isolation is, of course, crucial to the entire poem. A sense of guilt also begins to be experienced. The Ancient Mariner realizes that he has done 'an hellish thing'. The other sailors begin to turn on him, accusing him of killing the bird that made the breeze blow. They call him a 'wretch'. However, when the fog begins to lift the sailors change their minds. They now declare that the bird that brought the fog has been killed, and they say that it was right to slay him in this way.

Let us look at Coleridge's marginal notes. These notes are interesting and various. Sometimes they simply comment on what has been happening; at other times they give a deeper explanation of the action while, on occasions, they are also extraordinarily beautiful and add to the poetry of the entire work, for example, the note to lines 97–102. In his note Coleridge declares: 'But when the fog cleared off, they justify the same, and thus make themselves accomplices in the crime.' In other

The Rime of the Ancient Mariner – **Samuel Taylor Coleridge**

words, all the sailors share the guilt of the Mariner by saying that the murder of the Albatross was a good thing. The Mariner may actually have slain the bird but they, by condoning his wicked action, become as evil as he. For this reason the whole crew of the ship, and not just the Ancient Mariner himself, will be horribly punished.

This punishment is delayed for a while. The wind continues to blow, the boat continues to ride on through the Pacific Ocean. A sense of mystery and adventure accompanies the voyage. The ship and the sailors are going to places that no man has ever been to before.

> We were the first that ever burst
> Into that silent sea.

Once again we should appreciate that there are at least two levels here. The first and simplest level is that of an adventure story. But, as we have seen, the geography in *The Rime of the Ancient Mariner* is never simple. Although it exists on a very physical level, the world around man corresponds to the world within man. In other words, the 'silent sea' is not simply an undiscovered ocean; it is also a symbol of a previously uncharted aspect of the sailors' emotional experience. And, as we shall see, the previously unknown ocean is a far from pleasant place. The ship immediately becomes becalmed. The breezes cease to blow, the sails slacken and melancholy spreads over the ship. The silence becomes unbearable. The sailors talk to each other simply to break the awful quietness about them. Not only are they becalmed in an utterly silent and unknown ocean, a place that already strikes us with feelings of fear, but life also becomes physically extremely uncomfortable. The sky is hot and coppery; the sun is 'bloody'. We begin to feel that the ship and its sailors are trapped in some awful cauldron where they must suffer for their crime. They cannot move. Everything is hot, dead, inert. Rather than feeling as if they are on board a real ship, they feel as if they are stuck in

> a painted ship
> Upon a painted ocean.

But this is not all. The horror increases. As Coleridge's note tells us: 'The Albatross begins to be avenged'. The stanzas with which the poet describes this are some of the most famous in the whole poem and also some of the most powerful. Trapped in the boiling cauldron of this unknown sea, the suffering mariners become desperately thirsty. There is salt water around them but nothing to slake their thirst:

> Water, water, everywhere,
> And all the boards did shrink;
> Water, water, everywhere,
> Nor any drop to drink.

Note the simplicity and vividness of this stanza. The repetition of the word 'water' no less than four times suggests both the vastness of the ocean around the mariners and also their desperate need to drink. The irony is excruciating. The small detail of the boards in the boat shrinking with the dryness and heat reinforces the physical anguish that the sailors are suffering. Gradually this ghastly landscape begins to take on nightmarish proportions. The depths of the sea begin to rot in the heat, and 'slimy things' begin to crawl 'upon the slimy sea'. Again, the horror is intense. The repetition of the word 'sliminess' reinforces the idea of putrefying water, while the description of the monsters simply as 'things' suggests revolting forces of nature that cannot adequately be described.

Just as the sailors' lives once contained the joy, energy and love symbolized by the albatross, they now contain horrors that are all but obscene. To this obscenity is attached a sense of evil, of diabolic energy. The death fires dance round the boat at night and the sea takes on the lurid colours – green, blue and white – which Coleridge compares to 'a witch's oils'. Slowly the crew begin to realize that they are in the grip of an avenging spirit. Notice how the sailors do not come to this decision by a process of logical deduction; they do not think it out. This is a poem in which feelings and emotions dictate our experiences, and it is through dreams that the sailors come to perceive the truth of their situation.

Their suffering is made the more ghastly by their thirst. Where previously they had at least been able to break the silence of the sea by talking to each other, their tongues are now 'withered at the root', and the horrible realization that their dreams have brought them – the fact that they are under the power of a cruel, avenging spirit – cannot be communicated. Each has to suffer this realization in his own private and silent hell. All that the sailors can exchange are 'evil looks'. They turn their silent, accusing eyes on the Mariner – realizing that his action has destroyed them – and to make him fully aware of his guilt they hang the albatross around his neck. The second part of the poem concludes with the wonderful image of the guilty Mariner surrounded by his mute accusers, suffering alone in the nightmare ocean, the symbol of his guilt hanging heavily round his neck.

The boat remains becalmed. A long period of melancholy boredom sets in: 'A weary time! A weary time!' This sense of passive suffering is an essential ingredient of the poem and will build up to horrific proportions, but it will only be fully felt after one further event. The weary sailors glance out over the endless limits of the sea and become aware of 'a something in the sky'. Once before they had looked up to see the albatross flying towards them. It was a symbol of hope, life and love. What is flying towards them now is something far different. Again, Coleridge adds enormous energy to his poem by use of very strong contrasts. The 'something' moves ever closer towards them. At first it is a mere speck in the sky, then it looks like a mist and gradually, as it nears, it takes on a more defined shape, moving on an erratic, zig-zagging course towards them. The suffering sailors look at it in dumb fear and amazement. The Ancient Mariner, desperate to say something, bites into his own arm and, as his blood begins to slake his thirst, so he has the energy to cry out, 'A sail! a sail!' For a moment, as Coleridge's note informs us, the whole crew experience 'a flash of joy'. It is a moment of hope that will soon be destroyed. For a few seconds they all grin in relief but soon their smiles wither. Horror follows. The 'something' veering ever nearer towards them begins to take on the shape of a ship.

But what ship can it be that moves so violently through the sea on which they themselves are becalmed? Clearly this ship is something unnatural. It bodes no good. It will be a further aspect of their punishment and suffering. The sinister ship draws closer and closer to them and suddenly interposes its shape between the sailors and the sun. The horrible shape of its masts resembles the bars of a prison window. Terror grips the heart of the Ancient Mariner as he realizes that the ship is a skeletal hulk. But if the ship itself is a sinister thing, its two crew members are truly ghastly. The Mariner looks at the vessel and sees the setting sun glimmering through it and lighting up the two figures: the Spectre-Woman and her Death-mate. Here indeed are figures from the most awful nightmare. Clearly the ocean in which the sailors' ship has become becalmed is no longer merely an unknown sea invaded by adventurers. It is a horrific symbol of the Ancient Mariner's guilt. The spectre ship and its ghastly crew are aspects of the punishment he must undergo.

As always in the poem, Coleridge makes us *see* the horror. He begins to describe the two women who make up the crew. The first of the women is Death herself, the other a figure who seems even more ghastly.

> Her lips were red, her looks were free,
> Her locks were yellow as gold:
> Her skin was as white as leprosy,
> The Night-mare Life-in-Death was she,
> Who thicks man's blood with cold.

Let us examine this description in some detail. The first two lines suggest someone rather beautiful: a woman with red lips, lively looks and golden hair. Unquestionably there is something attractive about her, and yet how horribly this attraction is undermined by the third line. Beautiful though this woman may seem, her skin is 'as white as leprosy'. She is a lethal figure. What does she represent? Coleridge calls her 'The Night-mare Life-in-Death'. She is a figure of the greatest importance not only in the poem but in much of Coleridge's other work. She is a symbol of life drained of all meaning and joy. She does not simply represent depression or a vague feeling of melancholy. She stands for the human spirit at its most inert. She is the exact opposite of all the loving joy that accompanied the albatross. Far from being full of life, potency and hope, she stands for what Coleridge called in another poem:

> A grief without a pang, void dark and drear,
> A stifling, drowsy unimpassioned grief
> That finds no natural outlet, no relief
> In word, or sigh or tear.

It is a feeling compounded of utter exhaustion and panic, a complete spiritual deadness. Indeed, it is worse than death; it is a living death. Because the Mariner has shot the albatross he too must die in some way. Not for him the easy release of a true death, the mere ceasing to exist; he must suffer a living hell. This is decided by the two figures on the boat. They have been playing dice with each other for the Mariner's soul. While the game is being played, there is a chance that he may die naturally, but the figure of Life-in-Death wins the game and so the Mariner must go on suffering in appalling solitude until his punishment is complete. No sooner has the game been played but the spectral figure of Life-in-Death shrieks out across the ocean, 'The game is done! I've won, I've won!' The spectral ship vanishes with dreadful speed. The cursed Mariner is left to his fate.

He is desperately afraid. His life's blood seeps out of him. The stars go dim, the night grows thick. Instead of the hot coppery sky, we are now presented with a lurid seascape lit by the ghastly light of the moon. The Ancient Mariner sees the steersman's gaunt face. Slowly the sailors become animated. They turn towards the narrator and the last action of these speechless men is to curse him with their eyes. How powerfully this suggests the almost unendurable silence and isolation in which the Mariner will suffer. Then, their curses given, they drop down dead around him:

> Four times fifty living men,
> And I heard nor sigh nor groan
> With heavy thump, a lifeless lump,
> They dropped down one by one.

How well the ugliness of the words 'thump' and 'lump' express the collapse into death of these men. But we should pause to think. At least they have been given the release of death. Their souls fly out of their bodies. As they depart, so the sound that they make horribly parodies the sound of the arrow leaving the Ancient Mariner's crossbow to enter the body of the albatross. He is reminded of his guilt even as he is left alone amongst the dead to suffer the far worse punishment of a living death.

The Wedding-Guest is appalled by what he has heard. The question naturally occurs to him as to whether the Ancient Mariner is some form of ghost or spectre. The ghastliness of the Mariner's appearance seems to reinforce this idea. He has bade the Wedding-Guest sit on the stone beside him and placed his hand on him to restrain him. Now, as the young man looks at his hand, he realizes how ghastly a thing it is, how it expresses the suffering that the Mariner has experienced. The Mariner's body is also thin and brown, ribbed like the sand at the edge of the sea. The Wedding-Guest is desperately frightened by the 'glittering eye' that shines out from so spectral a form. The Mariner understands the young man's fear but tells him he is not a ghost, that he has not died. He has had to endure something far worse. As the note says, 'But Life-in-Death begins her work on the ancient Mariner'. What he has to suffer is an unbelievable isolation of body and spirit. The stanzas which describe this have a simple and dreadful power:

> Alone, alone, all, all alone,
> Alone on a wide wide sea!
> And never a saint took pity on
> My soul in agony.

The horror is made worse by the dead bodies of the sailors around him and the 'thousand thousand slimy things' that creep upon the ocean. He hates them for their mere existence 'And envieth that they should live, and so many lie dead'. Around the Mariner is the nightmare world of decay: a rotting sea, a rotting ship, the bodies of the dead sailors and the obscene things crawling on the water. He tries to pray but his heart turns 'as dry as dust'. He is drained of love and energy, while the eyes of the sailors – their bodies supernaturally preserved – continue to stare balefully at him. For seven days he is obliged to live with the hatred of these dead men while he himself continues to suffer his living death.

To be released from suffering such as this – a suffering compounded of guilt, loneliness, silence and physical pain – a very profound emotional change must happen. A rebirth of spiritual joy is needed. Coleridge hints at the quality of this in the note that he adds to lines 263–6. In the natural excitement of reading the poem itself it is easy to skip the marginal notes, but if we fail to read this one then we shall miss one of the most beautiful passages of English prose.

> In his loneliness and fixedness he yearneth towards the journeying Moon, and the Stars that still sojourn, yet still moved onward; and everywhere the blue sky belongs to them, and is their appointed rest, and their native country and their natural homes, which they enter unannounced, as lords that are certainly expected and yet there is a silent joy at their arrival.

If we let the beauty of this passage work upon our feelings, then we shall come close to understanding the change that is about to take place in the poem. We have seen that the Mariner has been left alone on the nightmarish ocean. The moon has risen and its light falls on the lurid faces of the dead sailors. It seems that the whole vast structure of the universe has been designed to increase the Mariner's suffering. And yet there is far more to it than this. The stars and the moon have their own beauty, and with appreciation of this there comes a sense of joy and hopefulness. Notice how carefully the images in Coleridge's note point to this. The despair of the Mariner is not everything. The moon and the stars move across the sky, their 'home'. The sense of security and peace that this word suggests is a marvellously rich contrast to the isolation and spiritual poverty of the suffering Mariner. Further, when Coleridge describes the stars coming 'home' at night like welcomed kings, the feeling of dignity and 'silent joy' is extremely powerful. Somewhere there is an emotional and spiritual richness to counteract the desiccated suffering of the Mariner. He must learn to love the physical world about him. He must break out of the isolation, the life-in-death inflicted on him by his murder of a living thing.

But the only living things about him left to love are the slimy creatures crawling on the water about the boat. At first their ghastliness and obscenity were one more means of harrowing his soul. Now, as he reaches the very lowest point of his suffering, so the Mariner begins to realize the fact that they are alive, that they move and exist, is in itself welcome. He is not entirely alone in the universe. He looks at the monsters again and their colours, once so lurid, now seem to him beautiful. He notices what Coleridge calls 'their beauty and their happiness'. In his ability to welcome any form of life around him and realize that its mere existence is holy lies the beginning of the Mariner's redemption.

> O happy living things! no tongue
> Their beauty might declare:
> A spring of love gushed from my heart,
> And I blessed them unaware:
> Sure my kind saint took pity on me,
> And I blessed them unaware.

This is one of the most important moments in the entire poem. The Mariner, who has destroyed life about him amd suffered appallingly for it, blesses the monstrous creatures for their existence. He is brought back into contact with the holiness of life and living. As Coleridge comments, 'The spell begins to break'. As the Mariner realizes that life itself is sacred, the spiritual deadness that had suffocated his soul begins to lift. The albatross about his neck – the symbol of his guilt – falls free of him and sinks into the sea. At last the Mariner can pray.

We have seen the physical world so vividly described in *The Rime of the Ancient Mariner* is both real and symbolic. It exists physically: the Mariner can stretch out and touch it. But we have seen also that it is an image of his own emotions. Similarly, the awful heat and dryness from which he has been suffering is both a physical pain and a punishment for his spiritual sins. Now, because he has made the first great step in his redemption, because he has learned to love life about him, his physical conditions will improve. He is able to sleep and 'by grace of the holy Mother, the ancient Mariner is refreshed with rain'. While he is sleeping, he dreams that the buckets on the boat are filled with dew. For the first time since the shooting of the albatross, he has a dream in which there is some hope. And it is not a false hope. When he wakes the rain actually falls. Our feelings tell us that this is far more than a welcome cloudburst that will help to slake his dryness. The rain is a blessing. It is a symbol that the heavenly powers are beginning to forgive him for the murder he has committed. How marvellous a contrast Coleridge creates between the stanzas that describe the Mariner's thirst (lines 135–8) and those in which he describes the man himself drenched with welcome rain (lines 301–4). And, as he is slowly and partially restored to life, so he 'seeth strange sights and commotions in the sky and the element'. The air about him bursts into life just as he himself does. Fire flashes, the stars dance, the wind blows and the rain pours down from the sky.

The Mariner's ship sails on through the storm and the dead crew around him appear to come to life again. In fact, as the note informs us, what has happened is that 'a blessed troop of angelic spirits' has been sent down to reanimate the bodies of the sailors. While there is a great sense of relief in the storm and the sense of life about the Mariner, there is nonetheless something slightly sinister about the whole episode. As the Mariner himself declares, 'We were a ghastly crew'.

Certainly the Wedding-Guest is frightened by the Mariner's story. Once more he thinks of ghosts and demons and wonders if the Ancient Mariner has been surrounded by evil spirits. The Mariner tells him that this is not the case and describes how, when the dawn rose, the 'spirits blest' clustered round the mast and sang as they left the bodies of the sailors to return to heaven. The description of the music is particularly beautiful. Indeed, sound plays a very important part in this poem. We might like to recall the 'whizz' of the arrow as it left the Mariner's crossbow. We may also recall how, after the death of the bird, the sailors spoke to each other to break the awful silence that had closed around them. This silence, of course, is part of the penance imposed on the Mariner. When this part of his suffering is over, a great storm breaks out. Now the sounds that surround the Mariner – the man who has begun to learn the sacredness of life about him – are beautiful and harmonious. They are a mixture of the heavenly music made by the angelic spirits and also the carollings of the birds about him. The whole passage is one of great joy after so much suffering.

Nonetheless, as we have seen, much of the strength of *The Rime of the Ancient Mariner* derives from contrast and, at the close of the fifth section, Coleridge creates one of the strongest and perhaps cruellest contrasts in the whole poem. After the Mariner's great suffering comes a moment of serenity. However, it will soon pass. 'The lonesome Spirit from the south pole', who is determined to take full revenge on the Mariner for slaying the albatross, has, as the note suggests, carried 'the ship as far as the Line, in obedience to the angelic troop, but still required vengeance'. What this tells us is that, although the Mariner has been partially redeemed by the suffering and penance he has undergone, he must suffer yet more. For the moment the malignant and revenging spirit moves the ship in a magical manner. As the Mariner informs the Wedding-Guest, the ship is moved not by the wind but by the spirit. Suddenly the movement of the boat is interrupted. It lurches backwards and forwards and then, 'like a pawing horse', it makes 'a sudden bound'. The violence of this sinister motion causes the Mariner to fall down in a faint. He does not know how long he is unconscious, but while he is in this state he hears the 'fellow daemons' of the Polar Spirit talking in the air above him. Again this is a most effective contrast. We have just been told of the sublime beauty of the music of the angelic spirits. Now we hear the cackling of the demons. One of them points to the Mariner and declares that he is the sinner who has shot the albatross, the bird beloved by the Polar Spirit. We have seen the suffering that this has caused, but the second demon with a voice 'as soft as honeydew' tells us of more suffering to come:

> The man hath penance done,
> And penance more will do.

The feelings of joy and peace that have been aroused in us are destroyed. Only through further suffering will the full significance of the killing of the albatross be made apparent.

The marginal note (the first in the sixth section) now informs us that the unconscious Mariner is still in the hands of supernatural forces: 'the angelic power causeth the vessel to drive northward faster than human life could endure'. Only when this 'supernatural motion is retarded' does the Mariner come to his senses again. It is night. The moon is shining. The dead men stand together on the deck of the ship. The Mariner's 'penance begins anew'. He looks across at his sometime companions and sees their 'stony eyes' fixed on him. He reads in their looks the hatred they still have for him, 'the curse with which they died'. The horror of this hypnotizes him so that he can no longer pray.

The guilt that surrounds the Mariner's destruction of the bird again becomes apparent. But, as the note informs us, 'The curse is finally expiated'. At first he is very frightened. He compares himself to a man walking down 'a lonesome road', so frightened in the dark that he dares not look behind him. However, a wind begins to blow. It fans his cheek and mingles 'strangely' with his fears. He is both terrified and hopeful, frightened by what he has experienced yet somehow sure that the new breeze is 'welcoming'. Standing in the refreshing wind he suddenly realizes that he is nearing home. At this point in the poem we may care to recall the very first moment of the voyage out (lines 21–4). Here there was an air of excited expectation, the feeling that the voyage would be a thrilling discovery of adventure. How wrong this expectation proved. By shooting the albatross the Mariner destroyed the very joy that he had hoped to experience. Now, after his appalling suffering, he 'beholdeth his native country'. The familiar sight of the lighthouse, the hill behind the harbour and the 'kirk' are very welcome and he sobs with gratitude. The boat drifts into the moon-lit harbour. The Mariner sees the rock and the church bathed in moonlight. As he nears home so 'the angelic spirits leave the dead bodies, and appear in their own forms of light'. This is a magically beautiful moment. Though the corpses of the lifeless crew lie flat on the deck around him, there stands on each one an angel. With a silent wave of their hands, the 'seraph-band' who have guided the Ancient Mariner and his ship back to port now leave him. They make no sound. Instead, in rapturous silence, they bid him farewell.

But he is not to be left alone. The silence of the angelic band is replaced by the noise of oars in the sea about him. The pilot of the port calls out to him and he sees the man and his boy rowing towards him. Such is the Mariner's profound sense of relief at seeing real human beings again that even the horror of the corpses around him cannot destroy it. As the little dinghy nears the Mariner's ship he sees that it contains a third figure. This is the hermit, the holy man who lives in the wood and whose righteousness is such that he will 'shrieve' the Mariner's soul. The power of religion and righteousness will 'wash away the Albatross's blood'. Only through true and loving religious faith will the Mariner be able finally to expiate his sin.

The seventh and last section of the poem opens with a description of the simple and holy existence of the hermit. As he and the pilot near the Mariner's ship, so the Mariner hears their conversation. The men are wondering what this strangely beautiful light — in other words, the angelic spirits — really is. The three men approach the ship 'with wonder'. They look at the warped planks and at the thin sails. The boat reminds the hermit of the skeletons of dead leaves that hang in the wood where he lives. This description may also remind us of the boat that the Mariner himself saw, and which carried the ghastly figures of Death and Life-in-Death. Just as this appeared horrific to him, so his own boat appears dreadful to those at home. Just as the Mariner was frightened by the apparition of the supernatural ship, so the pilot is afraid of the ship bringing the Mariner home. Only the profound faith of the hermit gives him the courage to row on.

As the pilot, the boy and the holy man come closer to the spectral vessel, so the water rumbles louder and louder. The eerie and fearful sound gradually rises to an explosion which splits the bay and causes the cursed ship to sink 'down like lead'. The stunned Mariner is thrown into the sea and rescued by the pilot. The little dinghy spins round and round in the whirlpool of horror caused by the final action of the Polar Spirit. The pilot shrieks, while the hermit, confident that the love of God is greater than the horror around him, raises his eyes to pray. The pilot's boy is driven mad by the dreadfulness of what he has seen, and the Mariner is left to take the oars of the dinghy and row it back to land. In his madness, the pilot's boy believes that the Mariner is the devil himself.

When the little dinghy finally reaches the shore, the Ancient Mariner earnestly entreats the hermit to 'shrieve' him. The evil which has so afflicted him must be cast out of his body. He must be dispossessed, an anguishing process. His body is 'wrenched with a woful agony'. As he suffers in this way, so he is forced to tell his tale to the listening hermit. In the act of confession, the Mariner experiences some sense of relief. To some degree his sins have been forgiven. However, so dreadful is the crime he has committed against life that he can never be fully forgiven. He can never again live a normal existence among his fellows. His dreadful experiences make him an outcast, and from time to time the horror of what he has experienced builds up so painfully in his brain that he has to recount his tale. As he wanders – half saved half damned – in anguish over the globe, so he speaks to those on whom he knows his tale will make a profound impression:

> I pass, like night, from land to land;
> I have strange power of speech;
> That moment that his face I see,
> I know the man that must hear me;
> To him my tale I teach.

This is a very powerful stanza indeed (lines 586–90). It suggests simply and most effectively the Mariner's sense of isolation, the hypnotic power with which he tells his tale and the absolute force he has over those to whom he tells it. The Wedding-Guest has been one of these hypnotized listeners. As the Mariner concludes his narrative, so the other wedding-guests leave the hall and move noisily into the garden. Their joys are simple, their happiness good and natural. Theirs is the life of ordinary people in an everyday world. How different they are to the Mariner, whose spectral figure loiters so close to their happiness. The Mariner now looks again at the Wedding-Guest and tells him what his story means. He tells him again of the intense isolation that he has suffered as a result of destroying life; he tells him of the absolute necessity of religious love and faith. To this man who has seen so much of demonic power and has been forced to suffer so terribly at its hands, the love and righteousness of true religion are joys far greater than that of simple human love. His great delight is to walk to the church, accompanied by other, happier mortals.

With these words the Mariner begins to bid farewell to the Wedding-Guest. Before he departs he insists that the Wedding-Guest understand the meaning of what he has undergone. The Mariner knows how dreadfully a man suffers when he is deprived of the company of other living beings. By being deprived of love and joy and goodness, the mariner has come to see how sacred these things are. He has told his story not only to relieve the suffering he still experiences, but to teach others the importance of what he has learned: 'love and reverence to all things that God made and loveth'. Only through love of life, through a direct and good relationship to all living things can a man truly be said to be alive. To love is to be blessed and to live in harmony with the Creator:

> He prayeth best, who loveth best
> All things both great and small;
> For the dear God who loveth us,
> He made and loveth all.

And, as suddenly as he appeared, the Mariner is gone. The stunned Wedding-Guest turns away from the happy celebrations about him. The Mariner's story has indeed affected him. The power of the language with which the story has been told has seized his heart; he has shared the Mariner's experiences almost as intensely as the Mariner himself lived them. No one who has encountered such a figure can remain unchanged. No longer for this young man are the simple joys and happiness of the guests at the wedding. He wanders away to consider his experiences.

> A sadder and wiser man,
> He rose the morrow morn.

The ending is profoundly ambiguous. The Wedding-Guest – at first a simple, happy and natural soul – has been deeply shaken by the story he has just heard. He can no longer live in the world as easily as he did before. Through the power of the Mariner's language he has been made to re-experience the horrors that the Mariner himself has known. He has also been made aware, however, of far deeper and more intense emotions than he knew existed. Like the Mariner himself, he is aware both of profound isolation and of great and redeeming love. His simple existence has been shattered. Like the Mariner, he is forced to live in a divided world of living death and supernatural joy. He will never be free from the hypnotic power of the tale. Neither, if they have paid close attention, will those who have read it.

The Eve of St Agnes – John Keats

The Eve of St Agnes is a fairy story set within the framework of folklore. It is a tale about ghosts and lovers, passion and death. As we read it we should notice how vividly Keats describes the physical world in which the events take place. Just as in *The Rime of the Ancient Mariner* the world surrounding the characters helped to make clear what those characters were experiencing, so in *The Eve of St Agnes* the vividness of the sights and sounds, colours and smells brings the action to life.

It will be helpful if we understand the particular significance of the Eve of St Agnes (20 January). It was an old belief that, by performing certain ceremonies before going to bed on this night, young virgins would dream of the man they were going to marry. In this poem the young and beautiful Madeline performs these ceremonies – exactly what they are we will describe in a moment – but not only does she dream of her lover, Porphyro, she actually encounters him and is swept by him away across the moors, away from the hellish house in which she is living. Her dream becomes reality.

The poem opens with a description of a cold winter's night. Keats immediately appeals to our senses. We feel how the owl, despite his thick feathers, is freezing. We sympathize with the hare limping and trembling in the frozen grass. We see the sheep huddled together for warmth. We experience the numbness that the old Beadsman feels as he kneels praying. Keats tells us how his breath condenses into little clouds of ice and floats up to heaven. These vivid sensations suggest on the one hand discomfort and pain and on the other age and religious faith. We begin to question where we are. What is this cold place where an old man prays alone? For the moment Keats is content to let us wonder. Yet we cannot help feeling that there is something sinister in this. Perhaps we are reminded of horror films we have seen where old monks are part of a macabre world.

As the poem progresses, so we watch the Beadsman rise from his knees, take his little lamp and shuffle back through the chapel. Notice how vividly Keats describes even this. The Beadsman is a frail figure. In the icy January night he wears no shoes. He moves slowly, silently, amongst the figures carved on the tombs around him. The sculptures take on lives of their own. They too are freezing in the winter night and are imprisoned behind the rails that protect them. Once they were glorious figures, now they are merely sculptured knights and ladies praying in silence. They are like ghosts. Keats strains our imagination to the utmost and he does this for a reason. We begin to feel our way into the strange and sinister world of the poem. Our imagination is alert, inquisitive, trying to make sense of what it is presented with. Our thoughts and feelings have been brought vividly alive.

But this is not so with the Beadsman. His imagination is not working at all. He is part of the dark, cold and lifeless world about him. He cannot use his imagination. His 'spirit fails'. He has no loving sympathy or interest in the world. He is part of death and decay. In the third stanza Keats tells us why. The spectral figure of the Beadsman moves on through the chapel, opens a little door and is suddenly confronted by sounds of beautiful music. If his imagination should respond to anything, it should respond to this. But the Beadsman responds to nothing. His death knell has already rung. He is either in the last moments of his starved and life-denying existence or already a ghost. Life is without joy. His existence is one of penance and suffering on a cold January night, a night traditionally set aside for visions of love. There are no visions for this man, however. Instead, he goes his sad and solitary way to sit among 'rough ashes' and grieve for the sins of the world. The sense of death and frailty that begins the poem is most important. It has set our imagination working and it will be in profound contrast to the other scenes that Keats has to describe later in the work.

In the fourth stanza, after the Beadsman has opened the door and heard the music, Keats takes us through that door, out of the chapel and into another world. Instead of the slow shuffling of the Beadsman, we hear of 'hurry to and fro'. Music bursts on our ears, the marvellous music of the 'silver, snarling trumpets'. And in the new light on the other side of the door we begin to use our eyes. We see the rooms beautifully decorated. They are 'glowing' for a party. In strong contrast to the scenes in the chapel we get a sense of life and colour. Look at the way in which Keats describes the angels carved on the cornices at the top of the columns along the hall. As such things are vividly presented to us, so we begin to realize that we are in a medieval world of romance and strange happenings. It is known as the 'gothic' world and it is amongst gothic ideas of love and death, colour, sensation and love that we shall be moving.

There now burst upon the scene the wonderfully dressed characters from medieval, gothic romance who have been invited to the party. Feathers, diamonds, wealth, music and happiness are the most notable characteristics of the guests. We see them briefly but vividly and then we dismiss them, for we are asked to turn our attention to one particular lady who broods with thoughts of love and hopes of the visions that the Eve of St Agnes will bring her.

We are now told of the folklore that surrounds St Agnes' Eve itself. We learn that provided they perform 'ceremonies due' in the right way, young girls will dream of the men they will marry. To be granted these visions they must go to bed without any supper and lie between the sheets without looking behind them or around them. They must pray with 'upward eyes' for the vision they desire to see. It is important that we remember these details, particularly the fact that the young girls must not look about them. If they do this, they will not see the visions for which they yearn.

For the moment the young lady – we learn in stanza VII that her name is Madeline – is brimming over with desire to perform the St Agnes' Eve ceremonies in the proper way. Note the strong contrast this makes with the people around her. They are swept up with the energy and delight of a party. She, on the other hand, stands pensive and alone, hopeful that she will be granted dreams that will give her far more pleasure than the rush and excitement of a mere feast. She is not part of the vulgar, noisy herd of guests, but a sensitive and refined soul set apart from the others. Her longings and her hopes make her someone special. She barely hears the wonderful music. She takes no notice of the gorgeously dressed figures around her. Though men, aware of her beauty, tiptoe up to her, she is oblivious of them. Her heart is 'otherwhere'. Amid the vibrant life of the party, she alone is quiet and prayerful. The hope of visions is more intense than all the life about her. In a few moments she will begin to perform the ceremonies of the Eve of St Agnes.

Let us consider Keats' writing so far. He has shown us a beautiful, refined young girl amidst a group of noisy and extrovert party guests. He has told us of her extreme beauty and he has also told us that what matters to her more than anything in the world is that she should be granted a vision of the man she loves. We are now introduced to this man. In true romantic fashion, young Porphyro has come 'across the moors' to save Madeline. Keats tells us that his heart is on fire with a young man's love. Later we will learn that he has risked death to be near her. For the moment, however, he hides in the dark places of the mysterious castle. We must imagine him intent but wary, begging the saints 'to give him sight of Madeline'. For the moment this satisfies him. He burns to gaze on her, to kneel beside her, worship her, touch her, kiss her, 'in sooth such things have been'. His courage mounts and he moves a little further into the dangerous castle. His enemies are all about him. The vulgar rabble, 'barbarian hordes' at the party, are his mortal enemies. Even their dogs would howl at the sight of him. This is a place of danger and imminent death as well as a place of love. Only two people in the entire castle have any friendly feelings for him: Madeline, who is totally unaware of his presence, and an ancient and kindly maidservant, an 'old beldame, weak in body and in soul'. Her name is Angela.

No sooner is she mentioned than Angela appears. We see and hear her shuffling along the dark corridors, supported by her ivory-headed stick. Porphyro moves out of the darkness and into the flaring light of the torch on the pillar beside him. At first Angela is startled, but she recognizes Porphyro almost immediately, seizes his hand and begs him to get out of the dangerous castle as soon as he possibly can. In stanza XII she tells us of the cruel and insane guests invited to the party. She bids him flit away from them like a ghost. But Porphyro will have none of it. He begs Angela to sit down and rest. She tells him again that the place is not safe and asks him to follow her.

In Keats' vivid description of the passage of these two people through the hideous castle we are given a strong impression of dark corridors and low doors. As Porphyro stoops through an entrance, the feathers on his cap brush the cobwebs that have gathered in the archway. The old woman mutters to herself, wondering at his bravery and the depth of his passion. Eventually they come to 'a little moonlight room'; it is cold, shuttered 'and silent as a tomb'. Once again Keats manages to create the sharp contrast between burning love and the silence of death.

No sooner are they in the privacy of the room than Porphyro begs Angela to tell him where he may find Madeline. He begs her by all the powers of St Agnes to tell him where she is. The mention of the saint's name reminds Angela of the folklore Keats has already explained. She thinks of the harmless visions that the beautiful Madeline will be granted. She imagines that they will be safe visions, mere fantasies. But she also looks at Porphyro and realizes what danger his very real passion has placed him in. She thinks how particularly dreadful his death would be were he to be murdered by his enemies in this hideous place while the woman he loves is dreaming of him. She is amazed by the force and bravery which love has given him. Again she thinks of Madeline. She laughs at the thought of the innocent fantasies that the young girl will be enjoying.

Porphyro, the ardent young lover, looks at Angela's shrivelled face as she chuckles to herself. Keats compares him to a little boy looking on the face of 'an aged crone' as she prepares to tell a story. But Porphyro does not look for very long. His passionate thoughts take hold of him again. His eyes grow bright. He thinks of Madeline performing the ceremonies of St Agnes' Eve and having mere dreams of him. How much better than dreams would be Porphyro's real presence beside her. He yearns to be closer to her. A passionate thought comes to him and flowers in his brain 'like a full-blown rose'. His insistent feelings tell him of the absolute necessity of seeing Madeline, of interrupting her dreams with his real presence. He suggests a 'stratagem' to Angela, begging her to lead him to Madeline's bedroom so that he may lie beside her.

At first Angela is horrified: she calls him 'cruel' and 'impious'. It would be far better for him to leave the castle. In the tumult of his passion Porphyro sinks to his knees beside old Angela and pours out his heart. He declares that his intentions are entirely honourable; may he be damned if they are not. He promises that he will not even ruffle her hair. He desperately declares that if Angela does not do as he asks her, he will arouse his enemies in the ghastly castle with the noise of his shouts and let them attack him and kill him there and then. Angela is frightened at the force of such feelings from this young, ardent lover bursting with life and love. She is but an old woman nearing death. She describes herself as 'A poor, weak, palsy-stricken, churchyard thing'. Once again Keats has drawn a powerful contrast between real life, real love and death and destruction.

Porphyro is moved by Angela's words. He calms down a little. As he speaks woefully and sorrowfully, so Angela comes to realize the honesty of his intentions. Though she herself is near the end of her life, she is still aware of the potency of love. She agrees to Porphyro's plan; she will lead him 'in close secrecy' to Madeline's bedroom. Here Porphyro will hide himself, gaze at the young girl's beauty and 'win perhaps that night a peerless bride'. While Madeline is dreaming of the man she loves, that very man will be standing in her room beside her. Madeline's dream of her perfect lover will merge into reality. Her dream will come true.

In stanza XX Angela prepares for this. She tells Porphyro how she will lay out a sumptuous feast in Madeline's bedroom and bids him wait while she does so. While he waits, Porphyro must pray. He must prepare himself for the holiness of the passion that he is about to experience. Angela hobbles away and Porphyro indeed prays through the 'endless minutes' while she is absent. Eventually Angela returns and, leading Porphyro 'through many a dusky gallery', brings him to the silent, silk-lined, innocent bedroom of the girl he loves.

Porphyro hides. Angela turns to go. She places her frail hand on the balustrade of the stairs that lead down from Madeline's bedroom. She is an old woman and she needs help. At this moment something crucial happens. You will remember how the 'ceremonies' that are so important a part of the folklore surrounding the Eve of St Agnes require that the young girl who wishes to be granted visions of her lover must go to bed 'supperless' and, just as importantly, look neither to left nor right nor behind her. So far Madeline has followed the correct procedure; but now, as Angela falters on the stairs, so 'like a mission'd spirit' and wholly 'unaware' of what she is doing, Madeline rises from her bed to help her old servant. Going to support the old woman, her candle in her hand, she turns and thus breaks the rules. Through a single act of human kindness she has forfeited the chance of the promised vision of the man she loves.

Madeline leads Angela down the stairs to the safety of the 'level matting' below. The charm is broken. A greater charm will follow. Porphyro must prepare himself to look upon the woman he loves. She, 'unaware' of what she has done, must prepare to confront him. Still half asleep, Madeline returns to bed. Notice how brilliantly Keats describes her passage through the dark castle. Our first glimpse of her is interrupted as she passes behind a pillar. Then we see her again. It is this fleeting impression of a woman passing along a colonnade that Keats conveys to us in the last line of stanza XXII. As Madeline comes back into the bedroom, so her candle is snuffed out; 'its little smoke, in pallid moonshine, died'. She closes the door, prepares herself for the longed for vision, and remembers that the 'ceremonies' which conjure up these visions require that she remain silent. Of course, she is quite oblivious to the fact that she has already broken the rules. Nonetheless, her heart is swelling with the hope of love. Indeed, it is painful to her.

Of all the stanzas that describe the physical world in this poem, stanza XXIV is undoubtedly the most beautiful. It is, at its simplest, just a description of Madeline's bedroom. But if we read into it more deeply, we shall see that its effect is very rich indeed. We are asked to look at the window in the little room. It has three arches and is richly carved with fruit, flowers and intricate knots. The three spaces are filled with stained glass. Each pane is diamond-shaped and the whole is covered with marvellous pictures made up of the sumptuous colours that we may remember from the windows of medieval cathedrals. Just as the window itself is beautiful to look at, so the language with which Keats describes it is equally sumptuous, particularly the vowel sounds. The final picture of the shield in the central window, surrounded by saints and blushing red 'with the blood of queens and kings', is marvellously sensuous. Where could so beautiful a thing be seen except in the imagination? It is in the imagination that we are now living. The moonlight pours through the stained glass and the fabulous colours fall on the form of young Madeline. It is a moment of extraordinary physical beauty and emotional suspense. We are made to feel something of what Porphyro feels. The richness of the language unites us with the pulsing emotion in the young man as he watches his future bride kneeling beside her bed. As Madeline prays, so the glorious colours from the window – the red and blushing shield especially – fall on her hands. Amethyst falls on a silver cross she is wearing, while yellow falls on her hair and seems to enhalo her head. Madeline appears to Porphyro as truly angelic – innocent and unbelievably beautiful. It is hardly surprising that he grows 'faint' at the sight of 'so pure a thing, so free from mortal taint'. When Madeline has finished praying she stands up, removes the gorgeous pearls decorating her hair, unclasps the jewels still warm from her body and slips out of her rustling dress. But, still believing she must follow the 'ceremonies' properly, she dares not look behind her. She does not realize that she has already broken the rules, or that the visions for which she is hoping will merge with the reality of her lover who is watching her. Still in a dreamlike state, she climbs into bed and falls deeply asleep again. In stanza XXVIII Keats describes Porphyro lingering in this 'paradise', staring at the dress and listening to Madeline's breathing. When this slows to the deep, regular rhythm of sleep, he creeps out of his hiding-place, crosses the carpet in the bedroom and peeps between the curtains around the bed where Madeline lies fast asleep.

There now follows a scene in which the sumptuousness of the physical world mirrors exactly the rich emotions in this lover's heart. While Madeline is still blissfully unaware of his presence, Porphyro prepares a rich banquet. The gorgeous cloth he throws on the table makes almost as powerful an impression on us as the beauty of the window by which it stands. But the last lines of stanza XXIX are important, too. We remember how old Angela has been led out of the room by Madeline and down the stairs to safety. Keats does not describe her leaving the lovers and wandering back through the grim castle; rather, he makes us *hear* her departure. He describes the opening of a door which brings the noise of the loud music of the party to Porphyro's ear. We are reminded of the outside world and of the danger that threatens Porphyro even at this moment of exquisite rapture. The door shuts again, muffling the music. Angela has gone. For a few precious moments Porphyro is alone with the woman he loves.

While she lies in her gorgeous bed, he proceeds to lay on the table all the food that Angela has left in the room, as she promised. We recall that one of the 'ceremonies' surrounding the Eve of St Agnes required that the young girl go 'supperless' to bed. Here is a banquet that has been laid out for such a girl. Having turned around once, she has already broken one of the rules. It was an act of charity – an admirable thing to do – but we know that it is the first stage of preparing Madeline for the moment when the longed-for dream will merge into the reality of the presence of her lover. With the rich food that Porphyro has laid out on the table beside her, there is a clear suggestion that the second ceremony surrounding the Eve of St Agnes will be broken. Stanza XXX, which describes the food, is an evocation of sensuous delights. Beside the beautiful, still sleeping woman are heaped the richest foods that the world can provide. The rich food also suggests the richness and splendour of Porphyro's passion. When the banquet has been prepared, Porphyro begins to awaken Madeline. He places his warm arm under her head and speaks to her. He calls her an angel, his heaven. He begs her to open her eyes. How subtle a moment Keats has created here. The young girl lying in the bed, having unwittingly broken the laws of the Feast of St Agnes, believes that she will only dream of her lover. She does not realize that by breaking the rules through an act of human kindness she has prepared herself not for a vision but for the real presence of the man who loves her. Still she sleeps. There is utter silence in the room. Moonlight falls on the 'lustrous salvers' and on the carpet. For some anguished seconds it seems that Porphyro will never be able to wake Madeline from her dream to the reality of his presence. Words have no effect on her. He turns instead to music. He picks up her lute, and we are asked to imagine the rapturous chords of the ancient love song that he plays for her. Music, more beautiful than mere words, begins to act its charm. Slowly Madeline is roused from her deep slumber. Porphyro sees that she is half awake, half asleep, and sinks beside her in an attitude of prayerful adoration. Madeline, in her half-waking, half-sleeping state, feels the image in her dream merge with the real man adoringly present beside her. Reality and dream, fact and fantasy, merge together in her half-conscious state.

As she slowly becomes more conscious, so the pain of her awakening confuses her and makes her cry. Then, as she finally comes to full consciousness, she speaks to Porphyro. Waking from her dream, she thinks the sound of the lute to be the sound of his voice. She compares the image in her dream to the reality of the man kneeling before her. The dream – timeless, pure fantasy – at first appears to her more beautiful than the reality of Porphyro kneeling beside her. In her dream his eyes were brighter. He seems to her somehow 'pallid, chill and drear'. She longs to return to the world of fantasy, of dream and illusion. She longs to sink back there with him but, as she sees how deeply upset Porphyro is by what she has said, so the image of him before her melts into the image she had enjoyed in her dream. Dream and reality, fact and fantasy, merge in a 'solution sweet'.

We have seen that some of the strength of *The Eve of St Agnes* lies in the strong contrasts Keats is able to contrive. We have witnessed a most beautiful love scene in which dream and reality have combined. Now we return to a harsher world. Keats describes the wind and the sleet beating on the window panes outside Madeline's bedroom. From a moment of great warmth and intimacy we move to an awareness of a far harsher world outside. Porphyro, newly aware of the danger surrounding him in the castle, tells Madeline that her happiness is no dream. She is his new bride. For a moment she is terrified that he will leave her alone in the Gothic castle. If he were to do so, she would die. Her fears, of course, are quite unfounded. The last thing Porphyro will do is to leave her just as he has won her. In stanza XXXVIII he expresses the enduring faith of the love he has for her. He feels like a pilgrim who has been saved from spiritual death by a miracle. The only thing that Porphyro wishes to do now is to escape from the dreadful castle with his bride. He bids her arise. He feels that the storm raging outside is a magical one, sent to help them. The 'bloated' party-goers will hear neither him nor Madeline as they escape from the castle. He begs her to run away with him.

Madeline does as she is asked and hurriedly prepares herself, frightened of the danger that lurks in the castle. Keats produces a marvellous sensation of suspense and intrigue as he describes the two young lovers stealing away through the castle. They creep down the dark, silent stairs, past the little lamps flickering by each door. They move on past the tapestries blowing in the wind while 'the long carpets rose along the gusty floor'. The young couple move like ghosts, 'phantoms', as Keats calls them. At last they come to the gatehouse of the castle. As further contrast Keats compares these young, beautiful people with the drunken porter in his lodge. Here he is a marvellous picture of a huge man sprawled out in his little room, 'a huge empty flagon by his side'. Only his dog is aware of what is happening, but the creature, so much closer to nature, seems to realize the truth and urgency of Porphyro's love for Madeline. He watches them pass, shakes 'his hide', but does not alert the household to their escape. At last they reach the castle gate, slide open the bolts, turn the key in the door and make their escape.

Suddenly we are made aware that we have been listening to a fairy story. All the events that Keats has described happened 'ages long ago'. The lovers have fled. But though they are now dust themselves, their love lives on. As for the other characters in the poem – the Baron and his 'bloated wassailers' – they have been shaken by nightmares and images of death. Angela too has died, and the shuffling, death-obsessed Beadsman who opened the poem sleeps, an unwanted ghost 'among his ashes cold'. Just as the poem started with the images of winter and death, moved to the scene of rapturous passion in Madeline's bed chamber, so it finally returns to the images of death with which it began.

Morte d'Arthur – Lord Tennyson

Morte d'Arthur is one of the most beautiful and evocative of the narrative poems discussed in this book. It is a combination of death, sadness and magic. The poem describes the last moments of the wonderful world of Camelot when it has been destroyed by treachery. Its hero is King Arthur who, during his long reign, gathered around him the flower of chivalry: the Knights of the Round Table, men who pledged their loyalty to him and went on many great and strange adventures. At last, however, a handful of them under Mordred have proved treacherous. The poem describes the last moments of Arthur when the final battle against Mordred's forces has been fought and Arthur has been defeated. The dying king's only companion is 'the bold Sir Bedivere'.

Notice how the long, sad sounds of the vowels of the opening lines of the poem suggest exhaustion and the end of toil. The last battle has been fought. Arthur and his men have been defeated; they have fallen 'man by man'. Only Sir Bedivere is left to carry his king to a little chapel close by. Just as the king is wounded and exhausted, so the little chapel is all but wrecked: 'a broken chancel with a broken cross'. Here is a place, sad but magical:

> On one side lay the Ocean, and on one
> Lay a great water, and the moon was full.

King Arthur begins to lament what has happened, 'the goodliest fellowship of famous knights' that has ever been known is now at an end. It has fallen apart. There will be no more talk of great deeds done; no longer the beauty and civilization that existed in his castle at Camelot. The very people whom he welded into a great brotherhood have helped to destroy him. The only remote hope is the promise the magician Merlin once made to Arthur that, sometime in the long distant future, he will come back 'to rule once more'.

For the moment, however, Arthur is too exhausted to consider this possibility. He has been fatally wounded and is wholly dependent on Sir Bedivere's help. He bids the knight take his famous sword Excalibur, and reminds him of the magical way in which it first came into his possession. He tells how on one summer's noon an arm rose from the bosom of the lake holding the mighty weapon. Tennyson describes the arm as 'clothed in white samite, mystic, wonderful', thus conveying to the reader the sense of holy and magical powers which will grow throughout the poem. Arthur declares that he has been a worthy possessor of the sword, but now he tells Sir Bedivere to take the weapon and throw it back into the water. The knight is then to return and tell his king what he has seen. The throwing of the magic sword into the lake symbolizes the end of Camelot, of the Round Table and all that these things stood for. Clearly the mission with which Arthur has charged Sir Bedivere is full of emotion and sadness at the final ending of the great and glorious days.

At first Bedivere protests that it is wrong for him to leave his king, but then he remembers his loyalty and declares that he will do everything that Arthur bids him. He makes his way through the little moon-lit churchyard, over the graves and down to where the sea-wind sings on the waves at the edge of the water. He picks his way with difficulty towards the shore and eventually comes to 'the shining levels of the lake'. He raises Excalibur over his head. The moon, suddenly emerging from a cloud, illuminates the hilt and the haft twinkling with diamonds and precious stones mounted in the 'subtlest' way. He is so dazzled by the sight that he cannot throw the weapon into the lake. Far better, he decides, to leave the precious thing concealed in the 'many-knotted waterflags' around the shore. He does this and strides slowly back to the dying King. Arthur asks him if he has done his bidding. He asks him what he has seen and heard. Loyal and torn with emotion, Bedivere tells him that he has heard nothing more than the ripple of the water in the reeds 'and the wild water lapping on the crag'.

Arthur turns to him, realizing that Sir Bedivere has failed to throw Excalibur far out into the lake as he was told. He criticizes him, telling him that he has been false to his nature and untrue to his king. He tells him that it is shameful to lie and bids him go and do as he first asked. Sir Bedivere returns to the lake and picks up the precious sword; once again laments that it should be lost in this way. He talks to himself. Again, he thinks it wrong that Excalibur should be thrown away, but he also knows that it is wrong to disobey his king. Yet what if his king has asked him to perform 'an act unprofitable, against himself?' Surely it is because the king is sick that he has asked him to throw the sword away like this. Clearly Arthur is not in his right mind. If Bedivere keeps the sword, it will remain as a memorial to Arthur's greatness to the end of time. If it is thrown away, 'much honour and much fame' will be lost. He argues for what he thinks is the best, but Sir Bedivere does not realize the full seriousness of the issues involved. He does not understand Arthur's deeper purpose. He has done what he thinks is right. Once more he hides the sword and returns to Arthur. When Arthur asked him what he has seen, Sir Bedivere gives the same answer as the first time.

Arthur is angry now. He berates Sir Bedivere and accuses him of treachery. He is deeply saddened that his command has not been obeyed. He thinks Bedivere wishes to steal the precious sword. Nonetheless, he gives him a third chance.

Once more Bedivere returns to the lakeside, raises the marvellous sword in the moonlight and this time throws it into the water. The arm 'clothed in white samite, mystic, wonderful', now rises from the moon-lit lake, catches the sword, brandishes it three times and then disappears beneath the surface of the water. The power with which Tennyson describes this scene – the quiet, rapturous magic of the vision – is both beautiful and awesome.

Bedivere now returns to Arthur and this time in answer to the king's question tells him the truth. What had to be done has now been done, and the king prepares himself for death. He bids Bedivere carry him to the lake. Bedivere looks at him through tear-filled eyes unable to speak. Instead, he bends down on one knee and, placing Arthur over his shoulder, carries him through 'the place of tombs'. Arthur murmurs in his agony. He bids Sir Bedivere walk more quickly. Bedivere strides on, his breath curling in frosty clouds about him, his own mental anguish driving him on. With the body of his king over his shoulders, he picks his way through the difficult, rocky landscape and eventually comes to 'the level lake'. Despite death and sadness, the scene is one of great beauty. Slowly that beauty merges into magic. A black funeral barge appears filled with stately black-robed figures. And, as they get nearer, so three gold-crowned queens raise 'a cry that shiver'd to the tingling stars'. Their sound of agony and lamentation rises like a wind in a waste land, a desolate place that has never been visited since the world was made. It is an awesome, primeval sound that echoes round the magical, sinister beauty of the moon-lit lake.

Arthur asks to be placed in the barge. The three queens stretch out their hands and, weeping, take him on board. The most beautiful of them lays the head of the dying king in her lap, loosens his armour, rubs his hands and calls out his name while her tears fall on his face. There follows the marvellous description of the dying king lying in the magic, moon-lit barge. To Bedivere the beauty and awesome sadness of this moment are unbearable. He cries out to Arthur, 'whither shall I go?' for he realizes that the whole glorious world that centred around Camelot is now ended for ever; 'the true old times are dead'. Where once there was adventure, loyalty, life for the living, now there is nothing. Only Bedivere is left utterly alone in the world to remember what has been. He will grow old, a man sundered from past glory, his days darkening round him. There will no longer be the glorious companionship of the knights, only isolation amidst 'new men, strange faces, other minds'. This is the poignant lament of a man who knows he faces irreversible isolation.

The dying king turns to Bedivere. As he is about to pass from the living world so he too has his vision. Where Bedivere can see only a bitter, meaningless life, Arthur can see more deeply into the future. He, like Bedivere, realizes 'the old order changeth'. Yet he realizes too that change is inevitable. 'One good custom' – the glorious life of Camelot – is not enough. It is simply not in the nature of the world to stay the same forever. It has to change, and, in changing, so it shows the variety of life, the variety of God. Only through such constant change and constant renewal can man come to know the infinite variety of God. Arthur now bids Bedivere pray for him. The religious vision becomes more intense. Man is infinitely connected to God. Prayer can do many things. Above all it connects man to God. It is prayer that shows man is superior to the animals, that he has a brain. He must use his brain to praise God, and to pray both for himself and for those around him. If man unites himself with God through his prayers, he unites the whole of the world to God, binding it together in 'gold chains'. In other words, prayer and love for the whole of humanity are the highest things that man is called to.

Arthur now bids Bedivere farewell. As he dies, his brain becomes clouded and unsure. He thinks that he is being taken away to Avilion, a heavenlike place –

> Where falls not hail, or rain, or any snow,
> Nor ever wind blows loudly; but it lies
> Deep-meadow'd, happy, fair with orchard-lawns
> And bowery hollows crown'd with summer sea,
> Where I will heal me of my grievous wound.

At the end of so much suffering – this vision of the end of the world as it has been known – there is some hope, some sense of a better place.

The funeral barge now moves away from the lakeside. The sails swell out like the breast of a swan, filling its lungs with air to sing its last most beautiful swan-song before it too dies. The poem finishes with the image of Bedivere standing by the lakeside remembering the past glories of life with King Arthur and the Knights of the Round Table at Camelot. So Tennyson leaves him staring out as the funeral barge diminishes in the distance, until 'the wailing died away'.

Morte d'Arthur is a poem about the end of a glorious and beautiful world. Although it describes defeat and death and verges on despair, so it also manages to show that the true purpose of life is loving companionship, faith and closeness to God.

Sohrab and Rustum – Matthew Arnold

Sohrab and Rustum is a tragedy that fills us with pity and awe: pity for its characters caught unawares in a dreadful web of unforeseen calamities, and awe that such appalling events should happen at all.

The poem is long and richly worked. Matthew Arnold reveals only gradually the full circumstances in which his two characters are placed, and it will be helpful if we start our discussion by making these clear. When we have a sure grip on the facts, we will be able to appreciate the drama with which the story is told.

Sohrab is a young, heroic warrior fighting for the Tartars against the Persians. Only late in the poem (lines 607–11 especially) do we discover the truth about his birth. He is the son of Rustum, the leader of the forces against whom he is fighting. Unknown to his father, who has been told that his only child was a girl, Sohrab has grown to become the flower of warriors. It is as such that we are introduced to him.

The work begins with a description of the dawn rising out of the River Oxus and the mists spreading over the countryside in which the two armies are encamped. Then we are introduced to the restless Sohrab. He has been unable to sleep. Clearly he is a troubled man for he has 'lain wakeful, tossing on his bed'. At first light he steals through the camp to the tent of his leader, Peran-Wisa.

Notice how Arnold's long sentences, some of them complicated in construction, nonetheless give to the whole scene a feeling of grandeur and mystery. We are being introduced to a strange and romantic world, one deliberately set outside of Europe and its familiar trappings. This strangeness is immediately attractive and provides an exotic background for the main characters.

When Sohrab has entered his leader's tent and woken the old man from his light sleep, he again shows us that he is troubled. He tells Peran-Wisa how he has been unable to rest. As he goes on to describe the mighty feats of arms that he has undergone, we begin to see that military glory, while it is something that Sohrab is well able to achieve, is not the thing that matters most to him. His troubles arise not from thoughts of the battles that will be fought, but from a more personal and private problem:

> I seek one man, one man, and one alone –
> Rustum, my father ...

Throughout the first part of the poem Arnold will present Sohrab as a young man deeply troubled by the absence of his father. Subtly and in many ways Arnold suggests how the young man's emotional needs – the problems which have kept him awake all night – are centred around the need to find his father and the love and security which he hopes to gain from him. The tragic irony of the poem lies in the fact that Sohrab will find his father only when, through the force of cruel and ironic circumstances, he lies dead on the ground before him. This sense of irony is of the greatest importance to the poem. In it lies the work's essentially tragic nature.

Sohrab now proposes a day's truce between the armies while he challenges the Persians to send forth their greatest warrior to fight him in single combat. Again, the reason that Sohrab does this is less for personal honour and renown than in the hope that when the challenge reaches the Persian lords 'Rustum will shortly hear it'. Clearly Sohrab is trying desperately hard to gain the attention of his unknown father.

Peran-Wisa at first tries to dissuade him from fighting. He declares that it would be much better if Sohrab remained within the army fighting with his comrades. Yet he realizes the strength and forcefulness of Sohrab's wishes. He also tells him something about Rustum. We learn that the man is old and no longer in the forefront of the Persian troops. Nonetheless, Peran-Wisa submits to Sohrab's wishes, telling him that he may indeed issue the challenge. But Peran-Wisa also feels a deep sense of foreboding. As he tells Sohrab, 'danger or death awaits thee on this field'. However, since he cannot restrain this 'lion's cub', he accedes to the young man's wish. Peran-Wisa's sense of tragic foreboding and the sense of doom generally that hangs over the characters in the poem is important, and near the close, when Sohrab has been killed by his own father, the dying hero will accept his fate. He will realize that there is no escaping the destiny that has been decreed for man: 'the doom that at my birth was written down/In Heaven' is something that Sohrab has come to accept. The cruelty, irony and tragedy, lie in the fact that his own father seals his fate.

The following paragraph (beginning line 94) is an example of how Arnold employs close observation to lend more life and immediacy to his characters and their world. It is particularly important in a poem dealing with the grand and tragic that it be rooted in this real world where everyday articles such as rugs, coats and sandals are in evidence. Such details help to convince us that the characters are real people living in a real world.

The next paragraph gives a powerful impression of the size of the forces under Peran-Wisa's command, but the details of the army are here less important than the language and sounds of words Arnold uses for his description. Matthew Arnold, who was a great classical scholar, knew that in the heroic poems of Greece and Rome descriptions of mighty lists of warriors contributed greatly to the epic effects that poets such as Homer and Virgil achieved. In this paragraph (lines 104–47) a similar effect is intended. The resounding, even exotic names, conjure up a picture of the mighty forces assembled. Only after Arnold has created this picture of massed strength does he allow Sohrab to utter his challenge to the Persians.

Just as the listing of warriors tries to recreate the heroic effects of the epic poem, so the following two paragraphs try to achieve the same. Similes are an important part of the work of Homer, Virgil and all epic poets. In an epic poem similes have to be of epic proportions. In *Sohrab and Rustum* they are often intensely beautiful also. Look at the simile in lines 154–9 where the mighty forces of the Tartar army are compared to a field of corn. The armed soldiers are as numerous and as packed as stalks in a cornfield. Arnold extends the simile. The soldiers are not simply likened to a field of corn standing in the sun, but to a field of corn blown by a breeze. This is a marvellous, exhilarating sight. Arnold compares it to the effect of Peran-Wisa's words on his army. Just as the wind blows through the cornfield so a shiver of excitement runs through the vast forces of the Tartars as they hear the challenge issued to the Persians. Note that in the course of the poem Arnold employs many more such heroic similes. Nearly all of them compare moments in the lives of his characters to great events in nature. Consider the effect that they have: they lend a tremendous sense of scale to the poem. The armies and the people involved in the work seem like forces in nature.

76 *Passnotes:* **Narrative Poems**

Inevitably, the mighty challenge issued by Sohrab worries the Persian forces. They realize that they have to accept the challenge and that they have no champion 'to match this youth'. Sohrab's military prowess is compared to a lion. The worried Persian lords cannot think what to do. Only old Rustum sitting sullenly in his tent, apart from the rest of the Persian army, is a worthy challenger. The Persian lords hope that he will 'forget his wrath, and fight'. Once again the tragic irony of the poem comes to the surface: Sohrab has uttered a challenge to the Persian army and the Persians – unaware that he is Rustum's son – can only suggest Rustum as a suitable warrior to fight for them. It seems that fate has decreed that father and son – unbeknown to either of them – will be forced to fight each other.

One of the Persian lords now goes to Rustum's tent and explains to the old man what has happened. Their desperation is clear when he says 'all eyes turn to thee'. Rustum is their only hope and this astonishes him. He protests that he is too old and then explains why he has set his tents slightly apart from the other Persians and the reason for his 'sullen' mood. The king of the Persians, Kai-Khosroo, is a young man who 'lets the aged moulder to their graves'. He will have nothing more to do with Rustum, and Rustum suggests that Kai-Khosroo or the young men that surround him should fight with Sohrab.

Rustum then explains his own personal unhappiness. He wishes above all that he had a son who was as fine a warrior as Sohrab. He believes that his only child is a 'slight helpless girl'. The irony of the situation needs no other explanation. Had Rustum a son as fine as Sohrab appears to be, he would willingly leave the army and go and look after his own old father. Gudurz – the Persian lord who has told Rustum of Sohrab's challenge – taunts him. He declares that men will say that Rustum is an 'old miser', a man too jealous of his reputation to risk an encounter with a younger man. The taunt succeeds. Rustum is stung into action. He declares that he will fight in plain armour so that he cannot be recognized. This is, of course, a most important feature of the poem, since the tragedy lies in the slow recognition of father and son after the fatal blow has been struck.

The next paragraph (beginning line 260) describes Rustum arming himself, donning his rich helmet and riding out on Ruksh, his horse. For all that Rustum cannot be recognized, we should notice the glorious sight he makes fully armed. Arnold uses another heroic simile when he compares the joy and relief of the Persians at the sight of the newly armed Rustum to the feelings of a pearl-fisher's wife when her husband returns safely home.

Earlier in the poem the Tartar army has been compared to a field of corn. A heroic simile is used again when Arnold decribes Rustum riding out to fight. Drawn up in squares, the Persian army looks like a field of corn when it is being reaped. As he steps out to fight, so Rustum sees Sohrab in the distance. He looks at him with intense curiosity. Arnold compares this, rather strangely, to a wealthy woman staring out of her window at a poor old soul going about her work. Rustum is moved by the sight of Sohrab, touched at the sight of such worthiness. The young man is tall, graceful and noble. Of course, the irony lies in the fact that it is indeed his own son that he is staring at although he does not know this. He does not wish to slay such a splendid young man. His natural feelings tell him that such a deed would be tragic. For the moment he does not realize how tragic.

Rustum at first tries to dissuade the unknown noble youth from fighting. He tells him that life is pleasant and 'the grave is cold'. He admits that he himself is a very experienced soldier who has never lost a fight. Pathetically, he bids Sohrab leave the Tartar army and come and live with him in Persia as his son. Sohrab is deeply touched by what he has heard. Just as the older warrior has paternal feelings for Sohrab, so Sohrab believes that the elderly warrior before him must be his own father. He runs towards him and, kneeling down before him, embraces the old man's knees. Something deep inside Sohrab convinces him that the elderly anonymously clad warrior is indeed his own father:

> Oh, by thy father's head! by thine own soul!
> Art thou not Rustum? Speak! art thou not he?

Rustum at first believes this outburst to be a trick. He thinks that the young man is, like all the Tartars, 'false, wily, boastful'; if he admits that he is Rustum, the young man will refuse to fight with him, will give him rich presents and then boast of how he challenged the mighty warrior, but so noble was he that he refused to meet him in single combat. Rustum thinks that Sohrab will have more to gain by showing his magnanimity, and therefore refuses to admit his true identity. Instead, he taunts Sohrab who rises to the challenge. Sohrab realizes that, now they are to fight, they are in the hands of fate. Fate alone will decide the issue of the combat.

> Pois'd on the top of a huge wave of Fate,
> Which hangs uncertain to which side to fall.
> And whether it will heave us up to land,
> Or whether it will roll us out to sea,
> Back out to sea, to the deep waves of death,
> We know not, and no search will make us know:
> Only the event will teach us in its hour.

Neither of the warriors realizes the tragic irony of their situation. Nothing more is said. Instead Rustum lifts his mighty spear and hurls it at Sohrab, who springs aside 'quick as a flash' to avoid it. When he launches his own spear, it is deflected by Rustum's shield. Rustum now picks up his club which, in a long heroic simile, Arnold compares to a tree trunk. Once again Sohrab springs aside; as the club comes thundering down it hits the earth and the old warrior falls to his knees. He lies prone on the ground before the young man, inviting Sohrab to take his advantage and pierce 'the mighty Rustum while he lay/Dizzy, and on his knees, and chok'd with sand'. The noble young warrior refuses so easy a victory. He bids the old man rise because, he declares, he finds it impossible to feel hostile towards him. He cannot explain his feelings. If the old man is not his father, who is he? How can his mere appearance prompt such deep and troubled feelings in the young man's soul? He begs his opponent to declare a truce. They should not fight, but rather, like friends, drink each other's health. As they do so, the elderly warrior will tell him about Rustum's deeds. Above all things Sohrab wishes peace 'betwixt thee and me'. The deep, unconscious feelings he has for the father he has never known render Sohrab all but incapable of fighting.

Rustum, however, will have none of such feelings. He picks up his weapons again and once more taunts Sohrab, calling him a girl, a 'Curl'd minion, dancer, coiner of sweet words!' The old man is determined to fight because he feels he has been shamed by Sohrab's attempts to make a truce between them. This fury rekindles Sohrab's hostility and the two soldiers fall upon each other like two eagles. The noise of their clashing shields is compared to the sound of woodcutters as they hew great trees with their axes. The fight now reaches its climax. Even the heavens are appalled by this unseemly conflict of father against son. A great cloud darkens the sun and a wind rises and moans across the plain, enveloping the struggling men in a sandstorm:

> In gloom they twain were wrapp'd, and they alone.

The horror of battle is so great that nature seems to hide it from the sight of the two watching armies.

As Rustum begins to get on top, so the sky grows even darker, thunder rumbles in the air 'and lightnings rent the cloud'. Even Rustum's horse utters a dreadful, unnatural cry that Arnold compares to the cry of a wounded lion. The watching armies quake for fear as they hear it. The river curdles. In the intensity of the struggle and perhaps hoping to gain his advantage, the old warrior calls out his own name 'Rustum!' The very word has the power to stun Sohrab. He shrinks back amazed as he hears the name, utterly bewildered. Perhaps, deep inside him, he realizes the true identity of his adversary. In his confusion he drops his shield and his father's spear pierces his side. The appalling and tragic deed has been done:

> He reel'd, and staggering back, sunk to the ground.
> And then the gloom dispers'd, and the wind fell,
> And the bright sun broke forth, and melted all
> The cloud; and the two armies saw the pair;
> Saw Rustum standing, safe upon his feet,
> And Sohrab, wounded, on the bloody sand.

Both armies are now aware that the fatal blow has been struck. Unaware of the tragic irony, however, Rustum taunts the dying warrior on the ground before him.

Sohrab looks up at the figure standing triumphantly above him. He declares that no unknown warrior has slain him, but Rustum himself. The unconscious power that his father's name holds over him, by disarming him mentally at a vital moment, has destroyed him. 'Something' about Rustum that Sohrab cannot describe seems to be part of this effect. The tragedy lies in the fact that Sohrab's own father has dealt him the fatal blow; there is great pathos in Sohrab's lines.

> My father, whom I seek through all the world,
> He shall avenge my death, and punish thee!

Arnold then compares Rustum to a mighty eagle who does not know that its mate has been killed. He is unaware of the full tragedy of the moment. He merely stands 'over his dying son' without recognizing him. Sohrab's words irritate him. In a 'cold, uncredulous voice' he says 'the mighty Rustum never had a son'.

After the physical disaster comes the emotional tragedy. Sohrab again looks up at his slayer and declares that Rustum indeed had a son: he, Sohrab, is that son. His dying wish is that news of his own death will eventually reach Rustum and make him 'cry for vengeance'. Nonetheless, Rustum's anguish on hearing about the death of his son will be nothing to the anguish his mother will suffer when she hears of Sohrab's death.

Rustum is 'plunged in thought' by what he has heard. He does not yet believe that it is indeed his own son who lies dying before him, and yet the suspicion is enough to alert him. He recalls that when his child was born he was away fighting and was informed that the child was 'a puny girl, no boy at all'. The child's mother sent this false news so she could keep Sohrab beside her and not have him taken away from her to be a soldier. The old warrior believes that Sohrab is lying when he says that he is Rustum's son, but tears come to his eyes as he looks down at the dying man and remembers his own youth, the love he had for his wife, and the perfect summer they spent with each other. He pities the dying youth and declares that Sohrab is just the sort of son he would have wished to have. His bitterness returns, however, as he declares that he has no son, only a daughter.

This angers Sohrab. He is near to death and knows that the words he is about to speak will be his last. He tells the victorious warrior that the proof of paternity lies tattooed on his own arm. Rustum's seal of a griffin has been worked into his skin and this is the proof that the dying warrior is indeed Rustum's own child. Horrified, Rustum begs to see the tattoo. Sohrab loosens his garment to reveal it. The full irony and tragedy of the situation now dawn on Rustum. He is appalled. He realizes that this fine young man is indeed his own son. His voice chokes. A dark cloud passes before his eyes. His head swims. He sinks to the ground beside his dying son, kisses him, strokes his cheeks and tries to call him back to life. He clutches at his sword determined to kill himself, but Sohrab, reading his mind, holds his hand and prevents him. The dreadful things that have happened have been decreed by heaven and there is nothing more to be done:

> Father, forbear: for I but meet to-day
> The doom that at my birth was written down
> In Heaven, and thou art Heaven's unconscious hand.
> Surely my heart cried out that it was thou,
> When first I saw thee; and my heart spoke too
> I know it; but Fate trod those promptings down
> Under its iron heel; Fate, Fate engag'd
> The strife, and hurl'd me on my father's spear.

The full tragedy has been revealed in all its awful starkness. All that remains for the mourning father and the dying son are a few moments of tenderness while life lasts. Rustum breaks down in tears and, as even the old man's horse seems to weep, so the two armies watch the tragic spectacle before them in awe. Rustum berates the horse for carrying him to the battle, but Sohrab — more tender-hearted in his dying moments — praises the horse and begins to imagine all the life he could have lived had he been united with his father throughout his brief but glorious life. Rustum, moved to even deeper regret, wishes only that he were dead. His son tells him that he must not die but rather go on living to accumulate for himself all the honour that Sohrab might have won had he lived. As he dies the boy asks his father to bury him with honour and with the following inscription on his tomb:

> *Sohrab, the mighty Rustum's son, lies there,*
> *Whom his great father did in ignorance kill.*

Rustum promises that he will indeed do this, and then is told by his dying son that he will only find peace when Kai-Khosroo is finally buried. In the meantime, it is the will of fate that Rustum, the slayer of his son, endure all that is sent to him. At last there is peace between the two men. Sohrab smiles, draws the fatal spear from his side and, as the blood wells out, so his spirit leaves him. The young man dies looking 'feebly on his father's face'. At the start of the poem we saw a mighty warrior deeply troubled by the need to meet his father. Now, at the close of the work, he sees his father but only with fading sight as he leaves the world behind him. Rustum, crushed by the tragedy that has overtaken him, sits in monumental mourning beside the corpse.

Night comes and the two armies begin to light their cooking fires; life goes on. The Oxus, the vast river of life, flows onwards to eternity while 'Rustum and his son were left alone'.

The Sacrilege – Thomas Hardy

The Sacrilege is a tale of passion, treachery, theft and murder. It concerns a beautiful woman, the gipsy who loves her, the gipsy's rival Wrestler Joe, and the gipsy's twin brother who is the narrator of the poem.

The work begins with the gipsy describing his love for a beautiful woman; so strong are his feelings that he promises her 'a silken kerchief crimson-red', the finest that he can obtain. This promise wins him the woman's love and, to honour his word, he sets off to Priddy Fair where he steals a kerchief for her. This buys the woman's affection for four weeks and the couple live together in the gipsy's caravan in complete delight. But after a month the woman grows restless and the man desperately wonders how he can win her affections forever. He describes her beauty as being 'bright as tulips blown'. Hardy creates a powerful image of the woman in his description of her drowsing in the gipsy's van, and how, when she looks at him, she heavily raises her 'sloe-black eyes' and murmurs to him in a soft sensuous voice. Herein lies her power over this man and she knows exactly how to use it. As he stands before her, encaptured by her beauty, so she declares that she will never again meet 'the Cornish Wrestler Joe' – the gipsy's rival for her love – provided he does one more thing for her. He must go to the nearby cathedral and rob the holy treasure chest of money to buy her beautiful 'ear-drops' and 'richly jewelled rings'. The gipsy is horrified at this. He admits he has 'gathered gear' – which almost certainly means stealing – for many years, but he has never stolen from a church. His conscience has told him that such behaviour is wrong. The sultry woman 'pouts'. So moody does she become and so terrible is the withdrawal of her love to the gipsy that he finally sets out for the city, bound to rob the cathedral's treasure chest. Just before he departs, he tells his twin brother the whole story of his love and begs a favour of him. He asks him that, 'should things go ill' – should he be caught and made to pay for his crime with his life – his brother is to murder the gipsy woman a month after his own hanging. The idea of her being Wrestler Joe's woman after his death is unbearable to him. His jealous ghost would never be at peace:

> My rafted spirit would not rest,
> But wander weary and distrest
> Throughout the world in wild protest:
>   The thought nigh maddens me!

The second part of the poem is told by the twin brother. He tells how he kept his ears open during the time of the theft, but only some time later heard that his brother had been caught and jailed. Just as the first part of the poem powerfully suggests the sensuous and languorous nature of the woman the gipsy loves, so the second part provides an exciting picture, described by the brother, of the gipsy being followed through the cathedral as he prepares to rob it. Here is a picture of a man warily doing something he knows is wrong and unaware of the fact that he is being observed. How vividly Hardy conveys the 'sacrilege' that provides the title for the poem:

> Yes; for this Love he loved too well
> Where Dunkery sights the Severn shore,
> All for this Love he loved too well
>   He burst the holy bars,
> Seized golden vessels from the chest
> To buy her ornaments of the best,
> At her ill-witchery's request
>   And lure of eyes like stars . . .

The evil beauty of the woman merges with the forbidden gold in the cathedral chest. Punishment immediately follows: 'They stretched him; and he died.' As the pathetic, condemned lover is dragged through the streets, so he whispers to his brother, begging him to remember his promise. The brother does so.

He describes how he shadows the woman just as her lover had been shadowed in the cathedral. Vengeance hangs over all the characters. However, the gipsy brother is a sensitive man and for a long time cannot bear to 'doom' so beautiful a woman. Indeed, he describes how, after the execution of her lover, the woman takes up with Wrestler Joe. There is a delightful description of the way in which Joe smartens up his caravan, painting it, hanging clean curtains and giving it a bright brass door-knocker. Evidently these efforts are sufficient to win this beautiful, feckless woman's love. Indeed, they seem to grow more fond of each other by the hour. The brother cannot help but sympathize even though he realizes that this is the woman who has been largely responsible for his brother's death. It is, he says, this thought 'that blew to blazing all my hate'. He now determines to fulfil the promise made to his brother. As it is the season of floods he decides to drown the woman. He continues to shadow her, getting closer and closer to her until he eventually speaks to her. His determination to revenge his brother makes him pitiless. He rounds on her beside the plank that is used as a bridge across the swollen river. He points across it to the hat and coat lying on the other side and asks her if they are her 'goodman's'. Do they belong to his brother or her new lover? The trapped woman blanches and begins to cross the river. As she does so, he tips the plank:

> ... She slid awry;
> And from the current came a cry,
> A gurgle; and no more.

The man has revenged his brother. There are no witnesses to the murder, no pointers to his guilt. But he has not got away with his crime. Vengeance comes full circle. He is haunted in his dreams by visions of the beautiful woman at the moment of her death:

> ... But in a dream
> Those ropes of hair upon the stream
> He sees, and he will hear that scream
> Until his judgment-time.

Hardy has written a poem as powerful and ruthless as any of the Border Ballads.

Lepanto – G. K. Chesterton

The Battle of Lepanto (1571) was one of the most important ever fought in the cause of western civilization. For many centuries the Muslim Turks had been threatening Christian Europe. Their empire was vast and powerful, but this heroic sea-battle finally secured Europe's freedom.

The poem opens with a marvellous description of the bizarre, beautiful and lethal power of the Turkish ruler, the 'Soldan of Byzantium'. Chesterton marvellously suggests his evil. Notice how the long lines – many with fourteen syllables – seem to curl round the man he is describing, just as the man's beard curls round his own wicked face. His ships have ventured as far as the Mediterranean – 'the inmost sea of all the earth'. They have even explored the Adriatic and the coast of Italy as far as Venice. Europe's rulers are in an anguish of terror. The Pope has called them together but they have taken no notice of him; Elizabeth I, 'the cold queen of England', merely stares into her looking-glass; the anaemic French king, the Valois, is listlessly unconcerned about the fate of Europe; the Spaniards are interested only in their overseas empire. As a result, the Soldan appears to have the upper hand: 'the Lord upon the Golden Horn is laughing in the Sun'. Only one man in the whole of the west has the courage to challenge him: Don John of Austria, a prince without a crown, and an insecure hold on his own lands, a poet and a man of chivalry. Chesterton's lines wonderfully convey the excitement of his preparations. In particular, notice that whereas the Sultan of Byzantium's laughter is sinister and fearful, Don John's laughter is that of a brave and extrovert hero. This man, though having little real standing among the other rulers of Europe, is nonetheless the hero who will save the western world.

The third and fourth stanzas of the poem are descriptions of supernatural evil. You may like to compare them to those in *The Rime of the Ancient Mariner*. The stanzas describe the devil and his servants.

Although it is quite wrong to think of the Muslims as devil worshippers, the effect that Chesterton wishes to convey here is one of absolute evil. In this he is successful. He describes 'Mahound' – a devil – lounging in the delights of his harem in heaven. It was widely believed by Saracen soldiers that when they were killed in battle they would be sent to endless bliss in heaven. Chesterton vividly portrays this paradise. He describes the devil Mahound's fabulous turban, the women who surround him and terror of his voice as he calls his evil angels to help him.

In the fourth stanza they come rushing towards us in a kaleidoscope of colour. Above all, listen to the sound of these lines and the way in which the long lines again seem to curl around about the objects they are describing in a sinister but alluring way. They seem to be part of the whole world: part of the clouds and the seas. The devils seem to bring with them a suggestion of enormous, indeed universal power. Nonetheless, as we shall see, this is only an appearance of power. These devils have no chance against the Christian heroism of Don John. Although Mahound commands them to break up the mountains and destroy the hiding-places of holy men, to remove all traces of the Christian saints of the world, it soon becomes apparent that these evil figures are confronted by a force far greater than their own. Where they are the agents of the devil, Don John, we are led to believe, is the agent of the true and all-powerful God. The noise of his preparations terrifies them. 'Four hundred years ago' – in other words at the time of the Crusades – they had been threatened by similar noises and similar heroes. The great men of the Middle Ages – Richard I of England and the heroes Raymond and Godfrey – had ridden out with all the power of Christendom behind them to smash the evil of the Turks. Now another hero has come to confront them. He does not believe in fate, in 'Kismet'. He puts his entire trust in God. At the end of the stanza we hear the noise of the drums and the guns that the great Christian warrior is levying against the forces of evil.

The next stanza is an important one and may at first seem confusing. If we are aware that Chesterton was a Roman Catholic and his hero Don John is a Catholic prince, we can understand Chesterton's wish to show in this poem how one great Catholic hero saved Europe from evil. This accounts for the poetry in lines 82–5. You will probably know that in 1571 the Reformation was taking place in Europe. Throughout the

Middle Ages Catholicism had been the only recognized faith. Many, however, regarded it as an increasingly corrupt institution, and in a number of different ways and in various countries men began to rebel against the authority of the Pope. They wanted to reform the Church, to set up their own churches, to worship Christ in their own way. This was known as the Reformation and in many cases the newly reformed churches only came into existence after a great deal of struggle, bloodshed and destruction. Far from wishing to worship God and love their neighbours, men quarrelled violently with each other over the meaning of the Bible. They were prepared to kill because of the differences that arose between them. This is what Chesterton is describing when he declares that the northern part of Europe – Germany and England in particular – are full of 'tangled things and texts and aching eyes'. Men have made themselves almost blind poring over the Bible and have neglected the real danger that surrounds them – the threat of the Turks. Instead of uniting against a common enemy, Europe has divided against itself. The people are no longer angry and surprised by the appearance of the Turk, rather 'Christian killeth Christian in a narrow dusty room'. Chesterton, writing as a Roman Catholic, takes this even further.

One of the many things about which people quarrelled was the degree of reverence that should be given to the Virgin Mary. Devotion to the Blessed Virgin Mary was and remains a central part of Roman Catholic piety. In northern Europe, however, the newly reforming Christians – the Protestants – chose to assert their independence by smashing all representations of the Virgin. Don John, in Chesterton's view a true and honest Catholic, far from indulging in mutually destructive activities such as these, puts on his armour and rides out to save Europe.

But if many northern European countries are interested only in fanaticism and mutual destruction, the greatest ruler of Catholic Europe is equally unable to save Christendom. King Philip II, ruler of Spain and its vast empire in the Americas, is presented as a strangely sinister and solitary man. Not for him the glory and action of war. He sits in his room, the Order of the Golden Fleece – the highest award for chivalry in Catholic Europe – hanging uselessly round his neck. Evidently this man is no soldier. Notice how Chesterton contrasts him to the active Don John whom he describes in the lines in italics. Far from being armed and pacing the deck, King Philip sits in a black-velvet-lined room, 'and little dwarfs creep out of it and little dwarfs creep in'. The neurotic Emperor holds a sinister 'crystal phial' in his hands. Perhaps it contains some sort of drug, for when he touches it his fingers tingle and he begins to shake. He is a sick and corrupt man. His face 'is as a fungus of leprous white and grey'. You may like to compare this picture of the Emperor to that of Life-in-Death in *The Rime of the Ancient Mariner*, for this sinister figure also had skin 'as white as leprosy'. While the sick Emperor's thoughts tend towards death and self-destruction, Don John is concerned with action and salvation. The battle has begun. The Catholic hero of Europe 'has loosed the cannonade'.

We return to a picture of the Pope praying in his chapel. He has a vision of the battle being fought. The vast and evil ships of the Turks seem to tower over the small vessels of the Christians. Chesterton's phrase 'the galleys of St Mark' makes it clear that the Christian ships are from Venice. St Mark, of course, is the patron saint of Venice, at that time a great nautical power. There then follows a vivid description of the power behind, or within, the Turkish ships. Deep within the dark holds of these dreadful vessels are the Christian slaves deprived of sunlight and freedom. Their life – so terrible that some of them are going insane – has been a constant anguish, but now there is hope for them. 'Don John of Austria has burst the battle line!' Victory is at hand. The Christian hero begins to wreck the Turkish fleet and the men who command it. The sea is red with their blood, and, as the Turkish vessels are destroyed, so there comes hope to the Christian slaves as they emerge into the daylight, 'white for bliss and blind for sun and stunned for liberty'. The hero has freed Europe. *Domino gloria!* 'Glory be to God', as Chesterton declares.

The last stanza of the poem is again somewhat confusing if we do not know the historical background. We have described the Battle of Lepanto as the great victory fought by the Christian forces under Don John against a savage, evil and alien power. This is the way in which Chesterton chooses to present the matter. However, we should remember – indeed we are told – that another very famous man was present at the occasion. For Cervantes, the great Spanish writer and author of *Don Quixote*, the Battle of Lepanto was very far from a simple and glorious victory. In fact, the great man was badly wounded in the struggle, losing all use of his left arm as the result of a wound he sustained in it. A man of intelligence and refinement, Cervantes realized that the violence and cruelty of the Battle of Lepanto marked the end of the old age of chivalry. Hereafter it was no longer possible to fight as the knights of the Middle Ages had fought. Battle was no longer a series of glorious encounters but a savage and dreadful business. The old codes of chivalry no longer applied. Cervantes pondered on their passing for many years. Deeply attached to the chivalric ideals that knights of the Middle Ages had espoused to show how out of place they were in the modern world he created one of the great figures of European fiction: Don Quixote. Chesterton refers to this figure when he describes Cervantes' vision of 'a lean and foolish knight'. Don Quixote is the idealistic hero forever thwarted by the real world. Chesterton describes Cervantes smiling kindly at the image of Don Quixote that emerges in his mind. We know that it is a kindly smile for it is totally different to the Sultan's.

The final line of the poem refers us back to Don John as he prepares to ride home. Earlier in the poem Chesterton had described him as 'the last knight of Europe'. But is Chesterton asking us to compare the hero of his poem with the hero of Cervantes' novel?

Is Don John's heroism itself already outdated? Will the 'modern' world have any time for its ideals, or will it simply laugh at them?

Themes and Characters

LANDSCAPES, SEASCAPES AND OTHER DESCRIPTIONS

The poems we have been looking at in this volume take us to many different places for a variety of different reasons. Some of the landscapes we are asked to investigate – those in *Michael*, for example – are probably familiar to most of us. Others, such as the wonderful place evoked in the opening of *Sohrab and Rustum*, show us regions probably remote from our experience but which appeal deeply to our imagination. Yet other landscapes, such as the world in which the ancient mariner is forced to suffer, are again parts of the globe we may never have actually seen: they are nonetheless so vividly described that we can appreciate how they suggest not just places on the earth but places in the heart as well. Let us look at these varieties of landscape in more detail.

In the opening of *Sohrab and Rustum*, which introduces us to a strange and exotic world, Arnold asks us to use our imagination. He describes the fog rising out of the mighty river and the manner in which the tents of the Tartars cluster along its banks like beehives. He carefully builds up a picture of a wild, open, and romantic place covered by vast armies. Throughout the poem we get a sense of the great spaciousness and remoteness of the landscape. However, by the close of the poem we see that these descriptions are far from straightforward. At the beginning of the poem, Arnold's description of the River Oxus helps us to build up a picture of the scene he is trying to outline, but by the time we reach the majestic closing paragraph of the poem we see that the Oxus represents something altogether special for Matthew Arnold. It is much more than a mighty river winding its way through an exotic landscape. It is an image of life itself winding its way through the world, here flowing fast and furiously, there divided and sluggish, and at last reuniting into one great river that flows into the sea. Perhaps we may think of the sea, vast and beautiful as it is, as an image of death and eternity. Just as the lives of the characters in the poem have wound their tragic course, so the great River Oxus winds its way through the landscape, eventually to be lost in the mighty ocean.

Water is indeed a frequent symbol of death in the poems we have been reading. For example, the sea in *Sir Patrick Spens* becomes the violent and terrible element in which the hero loses his life. Water is an important part of the landscape so beautifully created by Tennyson in the *Morte d'Arthur*. Here once more we are shown a defeated, dying man whose end will be closely associated with water. Arthur has lost the last great battle. The idealism of the knights of the Round Table has been shattered by civil war. The wounded king lies with his only companion near a moon-lit graveyard. He looks up and begs Sir Bedivere to take his sword Excalibur and throw it into the lake. A weapon with magic powers, the sword must, at the end of Arthur's life, be returned to an equally magical element.

Notice the romantic beauty with which Tennyson describes the lake into which Sir Bedivere is charged to throw the sword. Not only are we asked to use our eyes as we see the path that leads down to the water, we are also asked to stumble forward with the reluctant knight as he nears the water's edge. Finally we are asked to listen to the water in the reeds as it laps the shore.

The great concluding pageant of the poem also takes place on the water. When Sir Bedivere has returned to the lake for the third time and finally found the moral resolve to throw Excalibur into the water, the samite-clad arm of a woman rises out from it to catch the sword and take it into the deep. It is a moment of extraordinary imaginative intensity. We are asked to visualize something completely unknown but which appeals so deeply to our feelings that we cannot fail to be moved by it. The combination of moonlight, mystical beauty and death, all of them connected with the lapping water of the lake, is very beautiful indeed. The romantic melancholy, the strangeness and imaginative intensity, become even greater as the funeral barge approaches. The landscape becomes one with the intensely evocative events that are taking place in it. Death, a sense of universal sadness, and the most exquisite landscape combine to create an unforgettable moment.

Sense of place is also extremely important in *The Eve of St Agnes*.

The poems discussed so far have all been about death and defeat. *The Eve of St Agnes*, on the other hand, is a poem which begins with suggestions of intense winter coldness, graveyards and ghosts. But it rises out of this sinister and macabre description to present a triumphant evocation of sensual love. Very deftly, at the end of the poem, it returns once more to the gloomy world with which it started.

Notice how brilliantly Keats uses the macabre, gothic mansion in which the events take place to highlight the emotions he is trying to present. At first everything is dark, cold and sinister. We are in some sort of chapel, a lifeless place apparently inhabited by one old ghost and decorated only by the sculptures on the tombs. How powerfully this contrasts with the scenes of revelry taking place in another part of the house. Music, lights and rich costumes suggest a wholly different view of the world. The house suddenly becomes a place of youth and laughter – both of which are nonetheless rather sinister. Into this perilous world comes young Porphyro to woo his bride. We have seen death, decay, laughter and high spirits. Now, as we approach Madeline's extraordinarily beautiful bedroom, we are witness to the most sophisticated sensual pleasure. Look again at the description of the window in Madeline's room; it is one of the greatest richness. As we read stanzas XXIV and XXV, so we realize that Keats is more than describing a mere physical object. The adjectives he uses, the details he describes, the very lushness of his words, heighten our own responses. The feelings that these stanzas create within us – awesome beauty and pleasure – are exactly those Porphyro feels as he gazes upon Madeline in her bed.

However, having created this marvellous effect, Keats continues to work at different aspects of it. From the beauty of young love we move to a description of the dangers that surround it. Once more the strange, macabre building which houses Madeline suggests the peril that she and her lover are in. On the inside of the window is all the beauty and warmth of Madeline's bedroom; outside the winter wildness and the cold sleet create an entirely different picture. Between the two is only the thin mosaic of the stained glass. When Madeline wakes up and the Porphyro of her dream has become the real Porphyro who is standing beside her, so she prepares to go out into this world. The couple flee. Suspense and intrigue are suggested wonderfully by the way in which Keats describes the tapestries billowing on the walls of the long corridors, and the carpets that are lifted by the wind. Again the descriptions of place correspond exactly to the feelings of those living in it.

Finally, at the close of the poem we learn that all these events happened long, long ago. The characters have been dead for years. After awakening such intense feelings of sensuous delight, love and peril, Keats return us to the world of ghosts and graveyards with which the poem began. Just as the characters in the poem move between suspicion, the fear of death and sensuous rapture so the castle and the rooms within it seem to take on different characteristics to suit these changing moods.

Three more poems we have read also describe their various landscapes in ways that correspond to the emotions and conflicts of their heroes. *Peter Grimes* is a story of lovelessness, brutal violence and the intense isolation that surrounds its hero until he is finally sent to damnation. Notice how descriptions of particular places in the poem tell us something about Peter Grimes himself. His 'mud-wall'd' hovel suggests Grimes's own moral squalor through its slovenliness. However, by far the most effective use of landscape comes in the closing lines of the poem where, after the deaths of the boys, Grimes is forced to lead a lonely, haunted existence on the mud-flats. The two paragraphs (lines 171–204) contain some of the most powerful and original description of landscape in all the poems that we have discussed.

It is, first of all, a very accurate picture. The details are all perfectly realized: the tar blistering on the planks, the eels, the gaping mussels, the tuneless squawking of the gulls and the crooked races of the crabs are all described with the knowledge and familiarity of a naturalist. In their way, they achieve far more than might, for instance, a photograph or a well-filmed television documentary. Not only are the details carefully described, they are very selectively chosen so that they create a most powerful impression. We must ask ourselves what that impression is and try to describe it. Essentially, it is of a flat, ugly, unbearably dull world populated only by one human figure. That figure of course is Grimes. His evilness has made him a social outcast and, far from finding consolation in the beauties of nature, he is left alone in a world that oppresses his soul 'with misery, grief, and fear'. The interior landscape of this man – the sordid, brutal feelings that make up his life – are exactly at one with the weary landscape in which his own barbarity has forced him to live.

This appalling natural world is particularly appropriate as a backdrop to the supernatural horrors which now appear to Grimes. The ghosts of his father and the dead apprentices rise out of the brackish water which boils with the sulphurous fury of hell itself. Because Crabbe has described the landscape with such precision of detail and emotional truth, we are entirely convinced by the descriptions of the spectres which Grimes himself provides. It is easy for us to imagine how a man exiled to such a barren and sordid place, harried by guilt, despair and loneliness, should indeed feel this world closing in on him and threatening him with visions that eventually drive him mad.

Such a combination of guilt and hallucination is developed even further in Coleridge's *The Rime of the Ancient Mariner*. Here, the parallels between the inner state of a man's soul and the external landscape in which he is forced to live are exactly matched. Again, just as Keats in *The Eve of St Agnes* managed to convey a whole variety of emotions through his description of a single house, so in Coleridge's poem, descriptions of the sea enable him to convey a range of emotions that vary between the happy exuberance of a boat setting out on a voyage and the ghastly isolation and despair of a man left 'alone, alone, all, all alone' because of his guilt.

Notice how many different aspects of the sea Coleridge presents. At the start of the work we are shown the comforting safety of the harbour and the sunlight on the waves; but very soon we see a completely different image – an ocean packed with icebergs that crack and split – that frightens even as it exhilarates. It is into this sea – which combines excitement, natural fear, a sense of adventure – that the albatross comes to offer the mariners comfort. We may remember that the albatross is symbolic of love and a sense of community, the belief that even in the most extreme wastes of the natural world there can be warmth and affection. When the Ancient Mariner destroys the symbolic and natural presence of the bird, the sea immediately changes. Life goes out of it; it becomes deadly calm. The sun boils in the sky and the whole seascape becomes not just a fearful physical presence but an image of the guilt and shame in the Mariner's own soul. He has murdered something benevolent and must now suffer for this. The change in the seascape in which he finds himself becomes a part of that necessary suffering. Where the arctic ocean had been fearful yet beautiful, the sea in which the Mariner now finds himself is supernatural and ghastly. Hideous monsters appear out of it, 'death-fires' dance all night; the water itself boils in lurid greens, blues and white. The physical suffering this unnatural sea inflicts on the sailors is part of their punishment. They are parched, desperate men and, as the seascape reflects their communal guilt, so its supernatural awfulness becomes ever more dreadful. The sea becomes a place of spectres, of skeletal ships and deathly figures who gamble for the soul of the Mariner.

As we have seen, the Mariner is not allowed to die. He must suffer more. Once again the description of the seascapes will mirror the state of his own emotions and contribute to his punishment. As his companions drop dead around him, we glimpse another aspect of the sea that we have not seen before: it becomes an endless expanse in which the Mariner is an isolated figure. The endless wastes of the sea are an exact image of his spiritual desolation:

> Alone, alone, all, all alone,
> Alone on a wide wide sea!
> And never a saint took pity on
> My soul in agony.

In this hellish seascape the Ancient Mariner begins to learn about the truth of the physical and spiritual worlds in which he lives. Wholly isolated in this endless waste of water, deprived of human companionship and with nothing more than the monsters around him, he begins to see that even these repulsive aspects of life are holy because they have life. If changes in the seascape are one way in which the Mariner suffers, they are also a way in which he learns. Once he realizes that any form of life, however repulsive it may be, has something sacred about it, then his process of redemption can begin. The albatross falls from his neck; the hot air becomes bearably moist; his physical suffering begins to be lessened. As the process of redemption continues, so he is drawn with fearful, magical speed through the sea until at last he arrives back at the port from which he set out.

The lighthouse and the little chapel – the first buildings he has seen for a long time – are welcome and beautiful to the Ancient Mariner precisely because of their homely simplicity. Slowly he is returning to a world where blessedness is possible, where human beings can control the world about them and be truly united with God. It is here, when the Ancient Mariner has returned home, that the spiritual and physical experiences he has had on the ocean can finally be ordered and understood. He can be forgiven. After the appalling moment of his confession, he can return in part at least to the normal world and normal landscapes. But it *is* only a partial return. The world will never again be safe and comfortable for him; it can never again offer him peace of mind. Because of the dreadful experiences he has undergone, he remains forever a wanderer in an alien world.

Just as *The Rime of the Ancient Mariner* is a poem in which landscape and seascape are described not simply in physical terms but also in human terms, so Wordsworth's *Michael* is a poem in which landscape is of the greatest importance. It is not a soft, easy landscape but one of rugged beauty which forces a hard life on those who live within it. Nonetheless, it has a profound and beneficial influence on them, and inspires in Michael, Isabel his wife, and Luke, their son, strong feelings of virtue and contentment. It is very important that we realize this, for it lies at the heart of Wordsworth's poem.

At the start of the poem he describes his own attitude to landscape and his experiences of remote and beautiful places. Hills, valleys, farmhouses and windswept scrubby trees have taught him to see far more deeply into nature than books ever could. As a child playing in the hills, he fed his imagination on such surroundings. He came to realize that certain places – as that where Michael and his family lived – cause a bond between sensitive people and the natural world in which they live. Wordsworth puts forward this idea in his poem.

As we know, Michael and his family enjoy their rigorous life until it is threatened by financial worry. Michael has agreed to underwrite a loan for his nephew and, when his nephew's business fails, he is obliged to pay that money back out of his own slender resources. For forty years Michael has worked hard to build up and finally own the farm on which he lives. These years of arduous work have made him a stern but loving man, deeply at one with the landscape around him. He realizes he owes all that is best in himself to the natural surroundings in which he works, but, although he recognizes this bond, the depth of his love for the countryside is too difficult for him to express. He also knows that, given a similar background, his son will grow into a fine upright man. That is why he is so frightened when events make it necessary for Luke to leave home for the city.

Michael's deep, countryman's feelings tell him that the city is a place of potential wickedness and spiritual destruction, and he fears its influence on his son. Just before the boy leaves home, the father tries to impress upon him the spiritual beauty and moral purity of the countryside. He asks Luke to help him lay the first stone of the sheepcote which will protect their flock during the winter months. Michael knows that laying this stone is a symbolic gesture of setting Luke's moral and spiritual foundations in the countryside. It is also symbolic of Michael's hope that Luke will eventually return to this place. Michael believes that if evil and corruption should ever threaten Luke in the city, he will find salvation in thoughts of the symbolic gesture they are making together; he will recall all the goodness, integrity and honest hard work of his upbringing. But Michael's hopes are in vain. Luke goes to the city and, removed from the landscapes which fed his soul as a child, falls rapidly into evil ways and eventually has to go abroad to escape the law. The old man and his wife are left alone in the beloved landscape and the house which is so soon to be taken from them. Ties of family and land are not strong enough to save Luke, and the poem ends on a tragic note. The boy becomes a fugitive from justice, his father dies and is followed to the grave three years later by his mother. The farm is sold, the house pulled down, and only a few piled up stones suggest the pious hopes that Michael once nurtured – the hope that the beauty of the landscape in which his family lived could be powerful enough to save the moral well-being of his son.

LOVE

The narrative poems we have been discussing present love in a variety of ways. Sometimes love is romantic and magical, as in *Thomas the Rhymer*, sometimes gloriously beautiful as in *The Eve of St Agnes*. In Hardy's *The Sacrilege* it is tragic. Three poems – *Michael*, *Peter Grimes* and *Sohrab and Rustum* – present parental and filial love. Finally, in *The Rime of the Ancient Mariner*, we are shown the absolute necessity of recognizing the sort of love which is a universal bond between all living things and the groundwork of our whole existence.

Of all the ballads discussed, *Thomas the Rhymer* is perhaps the most tantalizing. Here we are presented with a picture of a poet, a fine man capable of standing up for himself, who is lured by the Queen of Elfland into seven years' thrall. This beautiful and mysterious woman appears to Thomas quite suddenly and clearly overpowers him with her sheer physical beauty. Her power fuels his desires and imagination and he becomes her helpless servant. When he breaks his word to her and actually speaks, so he is swept away into a beautiful and sinister world of enchantment. Possessed by a lady of the greatest beauty and magical power, Thomas is obliged to wander through rivers of human blood until he reaches her domain where he is kept captive for seven years. In some inexplicable way, beauty, violence, magic and love combine to create one of the most tantalizing poems we have read.

The Eve of St Agnes is one of the fullest and most beautiful expressions of a young couple's love for each other. In this work Keats deftly combines feelings of tumultuous passion and death. He takes us to the extremes of experience. He also shows us how dream and reality are inextricably bound up with each other in true love. At its simplest level, the story is compellingly romantic. It describes how an ardent young man, risking everything for the sake of the woman he loves, rides across the moors to the dangerous and sinister castle in which she lives and, finally arriving at her bedroom, wakes her, vows his love and then steals away with her. However, as with so many of the narrative poems we have been looking at, the poet has to do more than simply tell a story. Though the tale is a fine and compelling one, Keats enriches it with a whole variety of emotions and contrasts which make it appeal deeply to our imaginations.

We have seen, for example, how the poem begins and ends on a note of death. The rapturous, sensuous experiences that Porphyro and Madeline undergo are framed by images of the morbid and the sinister. Indeed, the poem opens with a vivid picture which contrasts strongly with young and passionate love: we are presented with a cold, dark chapel and a sinister, ghostlike figure who has no powers of the imagination, no ability to love and enjoy the senses of the body, no interest but for prayer and penitence, death, ashes and sin.

Because Keats presents such complex feelings so powerfully and appeals so deeply to our imaginations, the contrast between the opening scene and the mutual passion of Porphyro and Madeline is especially vivid. Madeline is young, pure, faithful and lives in a world of dreams in a house full of coarse, brutish aristocrats. Her very virginal purity is at once deeply attractive and an effective contrast to the ardour of Porphyro. For where Madeline is concerned only about dreams of the man she loves – Porphyro – that man himself is far more concerned about the physical reality of his feelings. He breaks into the strange, Gothic castle and, despite all its dangers, eventually convinces Angela to take him to Madeline's bedroom. At first the old woman is appalled by the idea. However, as she realizes the deep sincerity of Porphyro's emotions, so she realizes that she cannot stand in the way of such tumultuous, young passion. She must play her part in its fulfilment. She does so by leading the young man to his beloved's bedroom.

We have characterized Madeline as a beautiful young virgin. We have noted the different forms of love expressed in the poems under consideration. One such type of love is heady, romantic passion, another is sheer human affection. The latter is of the greatest importance in *The Eve of St Agnes*. The rules of the ritual to which Madeline has to conform state that not only must she go 'supperless to bed'; she must look neither to the side nor behind her. She must pay no attention to the world about her if she is to enjoy the dream fantasy. However, although Madeline thinks she has fulfilled these requirements, she crucially breaks one of them by unconsciously and automatically helping the frail, old Angela as she hobbles down the dark stairs. Still asleep, Madeline arises from her bed and takes the old woman's arm to help her down the stairs. Although the rules accorded to the ritual of the Eve of St Agnes have been broken, they have been done so unconsciously and for the best and kindest of reasons. However, Madeline will be able to enjoy her fantasies no longer. The spell has been broken. Through a simple act of human kindness, fantasy will be replaced by fact, dreams of Porphyro by his physical presence.

Keats describes this young man's passion with the greatest power and tact. Porphyro is obviously excited and physically aroused. Keats suggests the sensuous loveliness of young passion in his descriptions of the glorious richness of Madeline's bed-chamber, the rich and exotic feast and the music prepared for her, and by the marvellous vision of Madeline slipping out of her clothes and returning to the warmth of her bed. The richness of all this convinces us of the strength and passion of Porphyro's emotions. It is a marvellously suggestive and effective way of conveying love.

The music that Porphyro plays for Madeline eventually wakens her.

Her longed-for dreams are suddenly given reality by the real presence of Porphyro. At first the contrast between her illusions and the young man with whom she is presented is painful. Love triumphs in the end. Illusions and reality, dream and physical presence, eventually merge in Madeline's mind and, as the lovers are united in this way, so they become aware of the threatening world about them and steal away to a life of happiness and fulfilment, a life to which death comes naturally in the fullness of time. The rapturous passion of the greater part of the poem returns to the world of corpses and ashes with which it began.

The Eve of St Agnes portrays a joyous and triumphant love. *The Sacrilege* presents us with the tragedy often associated with passion. This poem is a tightly constructed little drama in which a beautiful gipsy woman blackmails her lover into committing a crime. She forces him to do what he knows is wrong: to raid the treasure chest in the local cathedral so that she can use the holy money for her own personal adornment. Notice the power with which Hardy describes the sexual allure of the gipsy woman. Her languorous body and sloe-black eyes are so compulsively attractive to him that, to keep her affection, he is prepared to do what he knows is wrong. His desperate passion leads to his death. He is caught red-handed and hanged, destroyed by the very love that seemed to give meaning to his whole existence. However, the tragedy does not end here. The sort of emotions that Hardy has been describing are deeply destructive. As the gipsy is being led to his execution, so he reminds his brother of his promise that if the gipsy gets caught his brother will avenge him.

At first the brother is reluctant to honour it. He realizes the great joy that has come to Wrestler Joe's life now that the gipsy woman has decided to live with him. However, so appalled is he by the thought that this woman has been directly responsible for his own brother's death that he vows eventually to avenge him and thus keep his promise. He shadows the gipsy woman, eventually catching up with her by a stream. He asks whose clothes they are that lie on the other side of the bank – his brother or Wrestler Joe's? The gipsy woman realizes that she has been found out, that the evil she has had the power to inflict has caught up with her. As she crosses the stream, the brother tips the plank and the woman falls to her death. She too is the victim of the disastrously destructive passions that she has managed to rouse. But there remains one final victim of this tragic chain of circumstances; the brother himself. Although nobody has witnessed the murder and revenge he has exacted, his conscience will plague him forever. Throughout the rest of his life and until the Day of Judgement itself, he will hear the woman's screams and see her 'ropes' of hair upon the stream. He too has been inextricably tangled in the tragedies of a destructive passion.

Three of the poems considered touch on the subject of the love that parents have for their children, and children should have for their parents.

In *Peter Grimes* we see what happens when a child refuses to love and obey. From his very earliest days Peter Grimes is shown as a person incapable of affection. Though his father deeply cares for him and tries to raise him in a decent God-fearing way, Peter rebels against this. From boyhood his life is devoted to hatred, vengeance and violence. He holds his father in utter contempt, refuses to comply with what he has been taught about proper Christian behaviour, and, eventually, in his evil and loveless state, lifts his hand against his father and kills him. Though his father once loved him dearly, his son's lack of response to this love leads the boy into a life of evil. We shall discuss this more fully in the next section.

Wordsworth's *Michael* is also a poem partly about the failure of parental love. Michael has brought Luke up in a severe yet kindly manner. He has trained the boy early in the ways of work and endurance, love and moral rectitude. These have been inspired in him by the landscape in which he lives. Wordsworth makes it very clear that old Michael's deepest feelings of affection are for his son. Although he is a stern father, he clearly adores the boy and does everything he can to bring him up to appreciate the best of the life that their existence can offer. He trains him to look after the sheep on the hillside, and he and his wife create for Luke a modest but secure home where the boy can be wholly happy. The depth of Michael's love for his son is most clearly shown when the two men are forced to part.

Michael's love for Luke expresses itself in two ways. First, he is truly afraid of the corruption which threatens the young man's moral and spiritual well-being away from the landscape in which he has been reared. Secondly, he expresses his love by asking Luke to lay the first stone of the sheepcote. We have already discussed the symbolism of this act. It is a deeply moral moment made all the more tragic by our knowledge that the sheepcote is never completed, that the boy does not return, that the father's love is ultimately ineffective. Sundered from the landscape in which he lives, thrown into the dangers and corruption of the city, Luke does not after all have the reserves of love and affection which can save him from moral corruption. For all the care that his father has cherished for him, the boy soon falls into bad ways, leads a life of dissipation, and is forced to leave the country. This tragedy lays bare a failure of love. Lost in the city, Luke forgets the deep affection his parents have for him and, by becoming corrupt, destroys the hope nurtured in him.

In some respects we can see *Sohrab and Rustum* as an opposite but complementary poem to Wordsworth's *Michael*. Once again the poem is the story of both a tragedy and a relationship between father and his son. However, where *Michael* shows us a young man forgetting his father's love as he sinks into the dissipation of city life, *Sohrab and Rustum* portrays a son deeply troubled by the lack of paternal love. Sohrab is a great warrior and a mighty fighter. He clearly stands out as one of the noblest soldiers in the Tartar forces he has joined. However, his bravery and excellence are undermined by the need to be recognized by his father and to have his love. At the start of the poem only Sohrab knows the truth of his birth: that he is indeed Rustum's son born while his father was away fighting and that his mother, scared that she would lose him early to the army, told his father that he was a girl. Sohrab proves he is indeed Rustum's child by the tattoo on his arm.

Sohrab has spent his young adult life fighting on the side of his father's enemies. Not only is he a mighty warrior but he is also a man whose psychological and emotional resilience is severely threatened by the need for a love which he has never experienced. At the start of the poem, this emotional gulf has caused him to spend a restless night. At the end of it he goes to the general Peran-Wisa and begs him to call a day's truce and offer a challenge of single combat to the enemy. He wishes to make this challenge personally, not to prove his valour, but in the desperate and rather pathetic hope that his father will hear of the challenge and so learn of his existence. The cruel irony of the poem lies in the fact that of all the Persian forces only old Rustum is a warrior of sufficient standing to take up the challenge. Unbeknown to either father or son, both men arm themselves for a battle in which the loving son will be slain.

There is something both deeply tragic and deeply wrong in a battle to the death between father and son. Even the forces of nature seem to recognize this, and as the fight takes place so its combatants are wrapped in a cloud of dust while the heavens darken over the plain beside the mighty River Oxus. The fight, with its taunts, challenges, blows and violence, is very powerfully described. It becomes perfectly obvious, as if proof were needed, that both men are warriors in the heroic mould. But it is not their physical prowess that decides the day, rather the magic aura that seems to gather around Rustum's name forces the issue. He himself has come to do battle anonymously so attired that his enemy will not know who he is. Nonetheless, when the older man is threatened and has to call on all his reserves of energy, so he shouts out his own name, for him a token of all his past great victories. For the father the name Rustum is a talisman, a word of magical power. For his son it is the exact opposite. It is a word charged with emotional significance whose very sound drains him of all his physical prowess. Sohrab is not defeated by a better soldier, but by the release of all the longing and emotional insecurity within him which is brought to the surface by the sound of his father's name. His aggression evaporates, the spear of the unknown warrior before him pierces his side and he sinks dying on to the sand.

Only when the physical catastrophe has taken place can the emotional tragedy of the two men's recognition of each other be revealed. As Rustum lies dying beneath the heroic and victorious figure of his unknown opponent, so the dreadful truth slowly comes out. The boy who has longed only to be loved and recognized by his father finds what he most desires in his dying moments.

In the same way, Rustum only recognizes the son he always wanted after he has mortally wounded him. The tragedy of the love of father and son for each other is inexorable, unavoidable. Sohrab himself recognizes that both of them are victims of fate. Though both have generous feelings for each other, fate has decreed that father should kill son. Rustum sits in lonely mourning beside the body of his child. Meanwhile the mighty River Oxus, the river of life, rolls on its way to the great sea of death and eternity.

Of all the poems we have examined, *The Rime of the Ancient Mariner* discusses love in the most universal sense. Underlying the whole work is the idea that an unquestioning and holy love for all living things is essential to our well-being:

> He prayeth best, who loveth best
> All things both great and small;
> For the dear God who loveth us,
> He made and loveth all.

The Ancient Mariner learns the truth of this by experiencing the terrible isolation imposed on him when he shoots the albatross. The albatross appeared to the Mariner and his companions at a time of great difficulty, their boat locked in an ice-bound ocean. That the albatross is 'a bird of good omen' is shown by the fact that the ice splits and the boat is freed as soon as the mariners receive the bird 'with great joy and hospitality'. Immediately after this the Mariner shoots the bird.

We should not look for a realistic explanation of this dreadful deed. It happens with the suddenness and irrationality that characterizes some of the ballads we have been discussing. It is far less important to ask why it happens than to understand what follows after the act has been committed. As we have seen, the Mariner is forced to undergo a long and excruciating penance. He has to be totally isolated in a hostile universe and wholly deprived of all love and companionship before he can fully understand the significance of the killing of the bird. Only when he has learned to love the repulsive monsters that rise from the depths of the foetid sea does his slow and partial process of redemption begin to take place. Eventually, as we have seen, he is 'shriven' for the sins that he has committed. He is at least partly forgiven and partly re-allied with the world of living creatures and men around him. However, it is important to realize that this forgiveness *is* only a partial one. Although the Mariner comes to appreciate the overwhelming importance of human love, community and religious faith, he can never live happily in the world of ordinary people. His memory of the dreadful things he has seen is so strong, his experience of desolation so total, that he remains forever something of an outsider.

It is also important to notice the framework that Coleridge creates for the poem. As we have seen, the Mariner recognizes through some sure instinct the people to whom he must tell his tale. He needs to recount to certain chosen individuals the horrors that he has been through, since, by telling them, he can ease something of his personal anguish. In this particular case he chooses a young Wedding-Guest. By laying his 'skinny hand' on the young man's arm and, through his sheer hypnotic power, forcing him to sit beside him and listen to his tale, the Mariner keeps him away from the happy ceremony. He isolates him, separates him from communal happiness just as the Mariner himself has been forced to suffer once he has slain the albatross. To be in the company of the Ancient Mariner is to be forced to experience the terrible depths of isolation and lovelessness which the Mariner himself has known. To those chosen people to whom he is obliged to tell his story, the events he recounts will be of a profound significance. Indeed, they will change the hearers' lives. Such people will be jolted out of their everyday, run-of-the-mill existences and be forced to learn things of terrible emotional power. At the beginning of the poem, the Wedding-Guest was an ordinary, happy young man. At the close he has been profoundly changed. We should notice that at the end of the Mariner's tale he does not rejoin the other guests – as he has often wanted to during the narrative – but instead he blunders away, confused and far less innocently happy than he was at the start of the work. Coleridge describes him as 'a sadder and a wiser man'. The Ancient Mariner sees in the young Wedding-Guest the ideal person to respond to his loveless tale. For the sensitive reader of the poem the effect of the mariner's recital is much the same.

CRIME AND PUNISHMENT

Many of the poems we have been discussing examine the nature of crime and punishment. Sometimes, as in *Jock o' the Side*, they do so in a light-hearted, even amusing way. We know that Jock himself is a rogue who has been involved in a number of border raids and skirmishes. We discover that he has been caught by the English forces and imprisoned, no doubt deservedly so. However, the anonymous author of this ballad is far more interested in stirring up within us a sense of exuberance and freedom as he tells us of the heroic, rather unlikely events, by which Jock is freed from the English prison, escapes imminent death and returns happily to his own country and people to sit in safety by their fireside.

In *Thomas the Rhymer* punishment is again inflicted on a man, in a magical and mysterious way. Thomas is a poet and a fine, upstanding individual who can speak out for himself. His tongue is his own, as he tells the Fairy Queen, and precisely because he speaks to her – despite being warned that to do so will result in his being her prisoner for seven years – he is swept away to Elfland in the company of this beautiful and bewitching woman.

Horrific and brutal crime and its punishment are the subject of *Edom o'Gordon*. Far from the light-hearted roguishness of *Jock o' the Side* and his border-raiding parties, *Edom o'Gordon* is the story of a marauder who inflicts the most appalling suffering on a defenceless woman and her family. Having failed to win her love, Edom decides to burn down her castle; when the woman's daughter begs to be thrown to safety over the wall of the castle, Edom's own spear runs through her little body. Although Edom is moved by the death of so beautiful a creature, he remains a savage and vicious individual, and we surely feel deep sympathy for the husband and owner of the castle when he returns to find it a smouldering ruin.

Of all the ballads that concern crime and punishment, *Edward, Edward* is the most stark and the most subtle. Only in the last stanza of the work are we told what has truly happened: a young man has murdered his own father at the instigation of his mother. The real subject of the poem is the slow, gloating and sadistic way in which the mother forces her son to confess that he has actually committed the murder. The drama of the poem lies in the remorseless but subtle cruelty with which the mother refuses at first to believe the excuses that Edward makes and then, when he has confessed to the murder of his father, the way in which she tells him of the penance he must undergo, the pain that he will suffer at being removed from his home, his family and, finally, from her. She manages to create for Edward a picture of his unhappiness. However, if he is to be punished by remorse and isolation in this way, his mother too will be made to suffer. At the very close of the poem Edward turns on her and spits out his curse. The man who was driven to murder his own father will certainly be punished, but the woman who made him commit this crime – his own mother – will also have to live with her son's curse ringing in her ears.

Thomas Hardy's *The Sacrilege* is similar to the other ballads in a number of ways. The language is, as we shall see (pp. 114–19), as direct and dramatic as in the best of the ballads. Its story is also constructed with stark and tragic clarity.

108 *Passnotes:* **Narrative Poems**

The poem shows us several crimes and several related punishments. Just as Edward in the border ballad was persuaded into murder by his mother, so the gipsy in this poem is persuaded into theft by his gipsy lover. As he commits the sacrilege – the robbery of the gold from the cathedral treasure chest – so he is caught red-handed. The processes of law immediately swing into action and for the crime he has committed the gipsy is hanged. No matter how much we may sympathize with the emotions that led to it, crime and punishment take their swift, inexorable course.

As we know, the gipsy has extracted a promise from his brother. Before he does the unholy deed he confides his plan to his brother and asks for his word that, if he is caught and punished, then the brother will exact revenge on the gipsy girl. This the brother eventually does. Although the woman is extremely beautiful and is now living happily with his brother's rival, he realizes that he must honour his promise and punish the woman. This he does by drowning her, punishing her for the way in which she lured his brother into committing his last crime.

However, if these two are punished for their acts – one through the course of law, and the other through another kind of justice – the brother himself is also forced to suffer for his own crime. For the rest of his life and throughout eternity he will be forced to hear the drowning screams of the woman and to see her image floating on the stream. For all three main characters in the poem – the gipsy, his brother and the gipsy woman – punishment follows the crime inexorably, and events enmesh them all in an inescapable tragedy.

Two further poems discuss the themes of crime and punishment. We have seen that the crime of the Ancient Mariner was to kill the albatross, and we discussed the punishment inflicted on him when we analysed his enforced suffering after he divorced himself from the world of love and living things about him. The other work which discusses the theme of crime and punishment is *Peter Grimes*.

This poem is a very subtle account of a man who, from an early age, seems to be damned. Indeed, Grimes appears only to be capable of criminal actions. At the start of the poem he refuses to accept his father's attempts to bring him up in a Christian, God-fearing way. But from being a rebellious youth, he rapidly deteriorates, becoming a murderer. He callously kills his father and thereafter leads a life of increasing isolation and brutality. He lives in squalor, works reluctantly and turns to stealing. But Crabbe is not only interested in outward manifestations of a criminal mind: he is interested in getting inside that mind itself. He wants to show us how a depraved man feels, to reveal the steady accumulation of horror and guilt that makes up Grimes's life. We begin to understand the pathological and criminal forces that drive this man into hiring a succession of boys whom he treats with appalling cruelty before eventually murdering them. We understand from this portrait of Grimes how crime and savagery feed upon themselves and seek ever more nurture. Crabbe's descriptions of the ways in which the three boys are forced to work till they drop, are beaten, starved and eventually murdered builds a sense of mounting horror and revulsion in us. We begin to understand the mind of a man who is wholly mastered by his need to destroy.

In some of the most powerful sections of the poem we also witness his punishment. This is vividly portrayed for us first by the descriptions of the dreary landscapes which, as we have seen, correspond to the sterility of his own heart and soul. Secondly, we experience Grimes's terror as he repeatedly encounters the ghosts of his father and the boys rising out of the water around him. Although we feel horror and contempt for Grimes – as well as a certain awe at the fact that a man can be so repulsively evil – we also, paradoxically, pity him as we learn of the punishment that he has to suffer. Pathologically evil though he is, we cannot but be moved as we see the pitiless way in which the ghosts rise in front of Grimes and drive him to despair and madness.

The moment when Grimes stares into the depths of the boiling water from which the ghosts have arisen and sees the eternal sufferings of hell is truly dreadful. In *Peter Grimes* Crabbe creates the most extraordinarily vivid impression of what it is like to be pathologically criminal.

WAR

Many of the narrative poems also discuss war and fighting. Two of the ballads – *Edom o'Gordon* and *Jock o' the Side* – are concerned with border skirmishes. In the case of *Edom o'Gordon* we see these in all their brutal horror, while *Jock o' the Side* shows them in a comic light. However, three poems discuss in a more complex way the issue of war and the death and defeat that inevitably attach to it.

In *Lepanto* Chesterton provides us with a battle between Christian and Turk, Europe against Asia. His canvas is large and, since the events he is recounting are part of history, he is able to enrich it with considerable amount of historical, even religious significance. We are first introduced to the seemingly invincible power of evil in a marvellously vivid description of the 'Soldan of Byzantium'. His sinister, wicked nature is suggested by the description of his beard, lips and unforgiving, inhuman laughter as he considers his imminent victory. The vitality and energy of his evil designs are also made clear as Chesterton describes how his galleys have scoured the Mediterranean and sailed up the Adriatic as far as Venice. Here is a depiction of a profoundly menacing and inhuman individual, but there is something irresistible about his energy and ambitions. This impression is reinforced when Chesterton describes the desperate, apathetic and self-obsessed rulers of Europe. None of them – the Pope, Elizabeth I, Henry IV of France or the King of Spain – seems capable of opposing the evil force about to be unleashed on Christian Europe. Heroism and chivalry, it seems, have died.

But in fact this is not the case. Though the great rulers of Europe seem incompetent or uninterested, one small and insecure ruler proves to be a hero: Don John of Austria shows that he is the last truly chivalrous knight in Europe. He is modest, kindly and talented, a poet and a man of action. Already he is gathering his forces. We hear the sounding of his drums, his trumpets and his canons. Where the beard of the 'Soldan of Byzantium' is sinister, Chesterton describes that of Don John as 'brave'. While the other Christian kings are listless and self-obsessed, we see Don John 'holding his head up for a flag of all the free'. Here is hope and activity – one good man pitted against the seemingly invincible forces of evil.

The third stanza introduces us to more of those forces of evil: the demons that belong to the diabolical 'Mahound'. These are the agents of the devil who hope to do battle with the forces of Christian good. The fourth stanza provides a powerful and effective description of them. They seem all-powerful, to be at one with the forces of nature. However, we come to realize that their power is not all that it might be, for those devils are frightened by the initiative shown by Don John, a Christian, Roman Catholic hero. He is at one with the Crusaders who fought the diabolic forces of 'Mahound' in the past. Don John has their energy and faith. He is the last in a long tradition of great Christian soldiers who have put the forces of evil to flight.

As we have seen (pp. 96–7), Chesterton ascribes great importance to Don John being a Catholic hero. The next stanza shows us an image of Northern Europe tearing itself to shreds in the anguish and violence of the Reformation. Far from uniting in a love of God against a common enemy, 'the North is full of tangled things and texts and aching eyes'. According to Chesterton, there is no sense of Christian love and common resolve amongst the Protestants. They have turned their backs on the good in religion such as the comforting presence of the Virgin Mary. The saviour of the western world cannot be taken from such a company. Don John, secure in his faith and resolve, is the man who will save Europe. Though he has only an uncertain claim to his throne, he is a far greater example of what a Catholic ruler should be than is King Philip of Spain, who sits in his black-velvet-lined room playing with a little phial of poison, shirking his responsibilities. While King Philip surrenders to his self-obsessions in his sinister chambers, Don John is fighting to save Europe.

We are now given a far more detailed picture of the galleys of the Soldan of Byzantium mentioned in the first stanza, ships that plough their way across the Mediterranean unopposed, and have even reached the northern Adriatic. We see that these evil and threatening galleys are rowed by a pathetic collection of emaciated and hopeless Christian slaves. A moving description of their suffering shows exactly the sort of intentions the Soldan of Byzantium has for the whole of Christian Europe. From such a dark and desperate position Don John succeeds in saving the Christian world. With his faith, energy and resolve he has managed to 'set his people free!'

Lepanto is a poem which glories in the triumph of heroic Christian resolve against the forces of evil. But in a disunited Europe, Christian in name only, one man alone has emerged as a hero, an exemplar of that chivalry with which the Crusaders fought. However, the last stanza of this poem which has so glorified medieval faith and chivalry asks some very probing questions about the nature of Don John's heroism. As we have seen (pp. 88–9), the Spanish writer Cervantes also fought at

Lepanto. He had witnessed Don John's chivalry and had realized that such behaviour is out of date. It will have no place in the new Europe to emerge after Lepanto. Chivalry will continue to be some thing enormously attractive but now wholly impractical. Cervantes was to encapsulate these contradictory ideas in the figure of Don Quixote, and we may like to think that Chesterton is drawing a comparison between his own hero and the hero of Cervantes' novel.

Tennyson's *Morte d'Arthur* is also a poem about the death of chivalry. Here we are presented with the end of the noble and idealistic world that focused on Camelot and its ruler, King Arthur. The Knights of the Round Table had been famous throughout the world for their virtue. Eventually the fellowship began to disintegrate. Arthur's wife proved unfaithful and a number of his peers under the leadership of Mordred revolted against him. A last battle has now been fought and Arthur lies dying, accompanied only by Bedivere.

The battle is over. Darkness has enveloped the world. We may like to think of it as the darkness of death as well as the darkness of the night itself. There remains only that ceremony which will mark the final defeat: the throwing of Excalibur into the lake to be caught by the outstretched arm, and the subsequent arrival of the funeral barge with its mourning queens. An atmosphere of profound gloom and suspense hangs over the whole work. To Bedivere, this atmosphere is almost unbearable. As he climbs his way down the zig-zag path that leads to the lake, so his heart is deeply troubled. As he lifts the beautiful bejewelled sword, the moonlight reflects on its ornaments and he finds it impossible to throw away so beautiful a symbol of the grand world that is now going out of existence.

He is ordered to throw the sword into the lake three times. On the first two occasions he is incapable of doing so. It seems so mean and treacherous an act, but his refusal to obey the command only heightens his king's suffering, and finally, on the third occasion, Bedivere obeys. Once he has described to the king the events that take place when he hurls the sword into the lake at the third attempt, the last rites can take place.

As Bedivere carries Arthur down to the shore, the profoundly melancholy scene is compounded by the king's suffering. As they reach the shore of the lake so the funeral barge appears in the distance. It is a luxuriously melancholy and beautiful symbol of the end of all that

Camelot has represented. Magical, melancholy and beautiful, the slow approach of the barge is like the approach of death itself. The lament of the ladies in the barge – 'A cry that shiver'd to the tingling stars', is 'an agony/Of lamentation.' It is both awe-inspiring and sinister. The queens take the dying body of Arthur, loosen his armour, chafe his hands and offer him comfort in his dying moments. Bedivere is left alone on the shores of the lake, the last good man in a decayed and hopeless world. His lamentation (lines 236–8) movingly evokes utter defeat. As Bedivere mourns the passing of such a noble life, his dying king offers him a speech of hope and love (see pp. 70–71). As he leaves the world, so he reveals to Bedivere the meaning and glory of life. This is to live in a way that unites the universe to God through love and prayer, to be sure of the fact that better days will return, and to trust that God's purposes are good. At these words the funeral barge moves off across the waters like a dying swan, and Bedivere is left alone in a dark world with only the king's last words to comfort him.

Of all the poems that discuss war, *Sohrab and Rustum* is perhaps the most ruthlessly tragic, a work about great armies and heroes which ends in the destruction of a son by his father. Throughout the poem, Sohrab is presented as a mighty, insuperable warrior, but one whose emotional well-being is undermined by the crying need to find his father and receive his love. Rustum too is a mighty warrior – the only hero among the Persian forces – but also a man deeply distressed by his longing for a son.

PARENTS AND CHILDREN

The theme of parents and children is an important one in several of the poems we have been examining. In each case it is presented in a tragic light. *Edward, Edward* describes a mother's sadistic fascination in drawing from her son the confession that he has murdered his father – at her instigation. The mother is portrayed as a tormentor of some skill and refinement, a woman who enjoys malice and evil for their own sake. In *Edom o'Gordon* a mother's anguish as she is forced to watch her children's gruesome death is related with stark, tragic power.

Peter Grimes also concerns the relationship of parents to children –

in this case father to son – but it is more subtle and complicated than the poems we have looked at so far. Grimes is a pathological killer completely lacking in human love and affection. Indeed, the poem opens with a description of the rebellious young Grimes scorning his father's concern. So violently does Grimes react against his father's benevolent interests that he strikes him down and kills him. Crabbe describes this action as 'sacrilegious', and it results both in Grimes's utter isolation from his fellow men and also in his growing desire to destroy the world about him. As we have seen, his evil nature precipitates him into an ever more squalidly savage world. As Grimes's crimes are punished at the end of the poem, his own father is principally responsible for this. Just as old Grimes has tried in his lifetime to show love and concern for his son – all of it rebuffed with scorn and physical violence – so now, at the close of the work, he remorselessly haunts his son and drives him insane with the images of guilt. The loving, Christian parent becomes the vengeful ghost who rises up out of the waters to show his son the hell to which he is propelling himself. Love, vengeance, crime and punishment come together to present a picture of inevitable damnation.

In *Peter Grimes* the destruction of the son by the father is part of the pattern of a remorseless justice. In *Sohrab and Rustum*, the destruction of the son by the father is part of the inexorable pattern of fate. Neither side is guilty of any crime but both suffer horribly. As Sohrab himself realizes in his dying moments, he and his father have been caught in circumstances not of their own making, and which they can do nothing to change. But if both men are shown to be mere puppets in the hands of fate, they are also in their own right men of great and even heroic stature. Though the father kills the son, both have an undying love for each other.

Throughout the work we have been shown Sohrab's attempts to be reunited with his father and to receive his love and blessing. We have also been shown the deep need that Rustum has for the son who he thinks has never been born. Both men feel a tremendous need for a deep relationship between each other, as father and son. We are left with the final tragic irony of their mutual recognition only after the death blow has been struck.

Wordsworth's *Michael* also presents the relationship between father and son. Whereas in *Sohrab and Rustum* the two men lived unhappily apart and were only reunited when Sohrab lay dying, in Wordsworth's *Michael* father and son live in harmony and affection. The boy is only destroyed when circumstances force him apart from his father.

Throughout the poem Michael is presented as a stern but loving parent, a fine, upright man who feels deeply the beauty and spiritual purity of the life he leads. He is a greatly concerned that his son should respond to the same things. Indeed, Michael's affection for Luke is the deepest love that he has. His care for the boy is most poignantly expressed in the grief he feels when Luke is forced to leave home. He knows the city will threaten his son's moral and spiritual well-being, and he does his utmost to try and reinforce in the boy's mind the love and purity with which he has been surrounded in his childhood.

This is symbolized by Michael's asking Luke to lay the first stone of the sheepcote with him. Despite Luke's upbringing, such symbolism eventually counts for nothing. As we have seen, he very rapidly gets into trouble in the city and is obliged to flee the country. Michael's hopes are dashed. His is the tragedy of a man whose love for his son fails to save him from moral destruction.

POETIC LANGUAGE AND FORMS

The full range of the narratives we have been discussing reveals an extraordinary diversity in the language and ways in which poems are constructed.

Amongst the simplest of all of these works are the ballads. This does not mean that they are the least effective; indeed, the opposite is true. Their very conciseness means that they get to the heart of their subject-matter with great power and intensity. Few of the poems we have read are stronger or more moving than the ballad of *Sir Patrick Spens*. We are presented here with all the necessary scenes of the story in rapid succession. We see the king feasting in his hall, Sir Patrick walking on the beach, the ominous moon, the storm and the drowning of the aristocrats. We also learn of the mourning of their ladies left alone in Scotland. A whole world of tragedy and destruction is presented to us with a terse mastery that is absolutely appropriate to the brutal subject of the poem.

This conciseness is typical of all the ballads. *Edom o'Gordon*, *Jock o' the Side* and *Thomas the Rhymer* present their stories in a terse way, but their very economy means that the events are sharply realized for us and are all the more impressive for being presented in basic outline. Notice how simple the verse forms that the poets use are. Most of the ballads we have discussed are in four-line stanzas which are either lightly rhymed or alliterative. Although they may be written in slightly unfamiliar language it is important to realize that this language appears to be the simple and direct language of everyday conversation. There is no attempt to be conspicuously beautiful or to be 'poetic'. Such unadorned language is sufficiently powerful and expressive for the poets to draw on and it was just these qualities that were also to appeal to a number of later writers.

John Gilpin, for example, is modelled on the ballad form. However, we should notice that it uses the simplicity of the ballads as a means of comedy. The jog-trot rhythms of the lines, the spare vocabulary and the simple verse pattern are intended to amuse.

In Coleridge's hands the ballad form takes on renewed life. He realized their true value. He knew that the poets who composed them were men of the greatest skill and insight, craftsmen who could pare their subject matter to the bone, present it in stark and simple terms, and so rouse powerful and genuine feelings in their audience.

Coleridge knew that the subject of the ballads was very often bravery, conflict, man locked in a sometimes desperate fight against circumstances. Their language and form was particularly appropriate to the subject matter of *The Rime of the Ancient Mariner*. Coleridge has a bizarre and wonderful tale to tell, a tale that is full of magic, drama and spiritual adventure. It is also a poem which expresses the most profound and awful sense of isolation and sheer despair. Part of the genius and craftmanship of Coleridge's poetic art is shown in the way in which he uses the ballad form to bring these emotions across. Like the poets of the ballads, he does not try to create something elaborate, wordy or ostentatious. Rather, he too pares his material to the bone, expressing it for the most part through a simple, if somewhat archaic vocabulary, and a verse form as directly understandable as that which the ballad-poets used. The effects he achieves are the same, perhaps even greater. Just as in *Sir Patrick Spens* the narrative moves with tremendous pace, changing from images of happiness to those of death and despair, so Coleridge's far longer poem tells its tale with great speed and dramatic effectiveness. And, just as the ballad-poets show us tragic events in their full intensity, so Coleridge, using the same simplicity and directness of language, can show us profoundly moving experiences. His figure of the Ancient Mariner knows he has 'strange powers of speech'. These powers are expressed through the ballad form he uses. He knows that his story has a hypnotic influence on those who are capable of fully understanding it. He knows that it has the power to change people's lives. The stark and simple forms of the ballad exactly suited Coleridge's purpose and style.

Thomas Hardy also recognized that the ballad was an extremely effective poetic form. Notice in *The Sacrilege* how although the construction of the stanzas and some of the language that Hardy uses is a little more complex than that found in the original border ballads, he creates the same powerful effects. How easily Hardy moves from images of great sensuous power – the gipsy woman's eyes, for instance – to a language exactly reflecting the natural conversational tones of his heroes, and so on to vivid images of ropes of hair floating in the stream, images almost as hauntingly dreadful to us as they are to the gipsy brother whose punishment they become.

But terse and simple language is not the only way in which a poet can achieve the effects he desires. Indeed, nothing could be more different than the language that the anonymous poet of *Thomas the Rhymer* uses to convey a sense of love and infatuation to that which Keats uses to portray the same theme in *The Eve of St Agnes*. Here the very lushness and acute, sophisticated sensitivity of the English awakens our imaginations to the most subtle range of experiences. Notice how at the beginning of the poem the limping hare in the frozen grass immediately appeals to our sense of vulnerability. How wonderfully evocative the scenes in the chapel are as they create a picture of darkening gloom, death, ashes and sin. The words have an immediate and compelling effect. We are drawn utterly into Keats's created world. But these opening scenes, with their coldness, darkness and macabre sense of death, are only a preparation for the far richer use of language in the rest of the poem. As we move further into the castle and see the lights and gorgeous costumes that are prepared for the party, so a sense of glowing wonder is awakened in us. This continues to grow throughout the poem until, with Porphyro, we are introduced into the heroine's bedroom, a place of a most rapturous, sensual beauty. The silks, carpets, the luxurious body of Madeline herself and the glorious, triple-arched window beside her bed, are described in language which brings the physical world before us with a vividness that we rarely discover in real life. The beautifully opulent stanzas, round vowel sounds and soft, lilting consonants are as physically exciting and as intensely beautiful as the things they describe. Here is a language of a most heady sophistication which exactly corresponds – indeed creates – the situation it is describing.

A far starker but equally sophisticated effect is created in *Peter Grimes*. Crabbe as an eighteenth-century poet used the heroic couplet, the great verse form of the age. This requires a highly contrived use of a line of ten syllables and, obviously, a very tight rhyme scheme. It is a most difficult form to use since it can appear both artificial and confining. Crabbe uses it with the proficiency of a true master. Though potentially contrived and restrictive, the heroic couplet here is a verse form of tremendous suppressed power and vitality. It can move from the brutal insistence of 'Pinn'd, beaten, cold, pinch'd, threaten'd, and abused –' to the sustained energy of Crabbe's descriptions of landscape, and on to the creation of the hideous and supernatural apparitions which drive Grimes to lunacy at the end of the poem. Precisely because the conciseness of the heroic couplet is so powerful, holding within it a force like a coiled spring, it can, when used by a poet of such truly powerful emotion as Crabbe, become a successful means of conveying horror and damnation. A verse form that is sophisticated, artificial and above all highly contrived, is here made the means by which appalling spiritual degradation and chaos are brought powerfully alive.

The ten syllables in the lines that Crabbe wrote are known as the iambic pentameter. This is one of the most common verse forms used by English poets up to the middle of the nineteenth century and it can be used with great variety. In Wordsworth's *Michael* it is a flexible form which can nonetheless convey a sense of massiveness: the scale of the mountains in which Wordsworth's characters live, the depths of their emotions. If we want to see something of the variety and effectiveness of Wordsworth's handling of the iambic pentameter, we might like to compare those lines at the opening of the poem which give so powerful an impression of landscape to those which describe the sudden and inexorable moral collapse of Luke. Where the opening paragraphs have all the breadth and spaciousness of the landscape and the emotions that Wordsworth is describing, the passage which tells us of the corruption of Luke is short, terse and, suitably, rather brutal.

Tennyson also uses the iambic pentameter line in the *Morte d'Arthur*, but the effect that he achieves is very different to the massiveness which Wordsworth wishes to portray. Here melancholy, magic, defeat and hope are the feelings he wishes to express. The situation itself – the dying king and the end of the glorious world that he brought into being – calls forth all of Tennyson's ability to create a delicate magical picture. Perhaps no other poet in the English language could use words so subtly and so evocatively, above all with such a various and sophisticated sense of their music. There is a sense of doom and sorrow in the very sound of the language, and it is in most effective contrast to the magic with which Tennyson partly relieves this sense of foreboding. The description of the samite-clad arm, of Excalibur twinkling in the moonlight and, above all, the funeral barge and its wailing mourners as it nears the edge of the lake are all superbly effective. We are asked to use our eyes and our ears, while the metaphors and similes with which Tennyson enriches the description only deepen that subtle combination of death and mystical beauty which is the subject of the work. Yet although the poem appeals deeply to our imaginations, making us visualize with the utmost acuteness things we could never possibly have seen – and in this lies much of its fascination – the physical description of ordinary nature in the poem is also most effective and helps to root the supernatural in the carefully observed natural world. Look, for example, at the description of the pathway along which Sir Bedivere has to pick his way to reach the edge of the lake. Listen to Tennyson's description of the wind in the reeds and the effect of the moonlight on the landscape as a whole.

We have seen that the iambic pentameter is capable of conveying a sense of massiveness. This is particularly true of Matthew Arnold's *Sohrab and Rustum*. As we have said, Arnold is trying to create here a heroic effect similar to the epic poems of Homer and Virgil. The sounds of the exotic names that he uses, particularly his great list of warriors help to create this as do the many images that he employs. You may remember the way in which he compares the armies to fields of corn blown by the wind. Particularly effective in the poem is Matthew

Arnold's use of heroic similes, extended comparisons between something which is actually a part of the narrative itself and something which Arnold is imagining. Look for example at the lines where Arnold compares the feelings that Rustum has immediately after he has slain his son to the description of an eagle that has lost his mate. Here splendid heroic men are compared to equally splendid birds smitten with a grief they do not yet understand. The effect is immediately to lend grandeur and pathos to the poem, and also a sense of man's belonging to the natural order of things. Finally, for a supreme example of the grandeur which Arnold can pack into his lines, look at the closing paragraph of the poem. As we have said, the description of the River Oxus is both factual and metaphorical, both a description of the actual river and also of the river of life flowing on to the sea of death and eternity. The description conveys exactly that feeling of life following its pre-ordained way through the world and eventually issuing into death. Just as both Sohrab and Rustum have lived their lives under the hand of fate and Sohrab has eventually died, so the river of life – the Oxus – winds its way through the vast wilderness of central Asia, finally to lose itself in the Aral Sea.

One final poem shows the range of language and verse forms that the poets we have been discussing can use. Chesterton's *Lepanto* is a poem in which rhythm is used with the greatest effect. Notice how the long lines of the poem draw the reader into the descriptions, convincing him of the evil of the Soldan of Byzantium, the seemingly universal power of the evil spirits attendant on Mahound, and the various forms of inadequacy personified in all the rulers of Europe except Don John himself. Notice, finally, how the short lines at the end of the stanzas suggest a sense of triumph and exhilaration. Chesterton's language varies from the simple to the complex and his verse form is of the greatest flexibility. If we compare it to the terse simplicity of the ballads, we can see the full range of the poetic language and poetic forms that these narrative poets use.

Glossary

Affrayed: excited
Agency: assistance
Agues: fevers
Ahint: behind
Ain Jock, the Laird's: Jock son of Lord Mangerton
Amain: with force, in haste
Anes: once
Argent: silver
Argosy: a romantic name for a merchant ship
Arras: tapestry
Attainted: corrupted
Averred: swore
Azure: blue

Balmy: warm, sweet and tender
Beadsman: one who spends his life in prayer
Beldame: woman
Billie: comrade
Botchery: letting things go wrong
bootless: luckless
Brae: stream
Braid: long
Brand: sword
Branks: halter
Brecham: straw collar
Bruited: made into loud common gossip
Burgher: a leading citizen
Busk and boon: prepare to go
Busket: dressed

Calender: a merchant selling fine, expensive cloth
Carol: a song
Carp: sing, recite
Casque: helmet
Cates: cakes and sweet things to eat
Chaise: a light, swift coach
Chancel: area of a church around the altar
Charnel: place where dead bodies are kept
Chased: engraved
Clarion: a trumpet call
Clave: clung
Clove: cut
Conceit: an elaborate idea
Coppice: a small wood
Corn-caugers: corn merchants
Cornice: moulding on the wall below the ceiling
Corse: corpse, dead body
Craven: cowardly
Crescent: a curved shape, like the new moon
Cuisses: body armour, breast-plate

Dam: mother
Daunton: cast down
Dew-beads: sweat
Dight: dress decorated
Dissolute: loose-living
Distemper'd: shaken with a fever
Dought: dare
Dule ye drie: grief you are suffering

Eftsoons: at once
Eke: also
Ells (three): over nine feet
Emblazonings: heraldic designs
Eremite: a hermit, one who longs for heaven
Escutcheon: a coat of arms
Execrations: oaths
Expiated: eradicate guilt

Faerily: magically
Fealty: loyalty, duty
Ferlie: marvel
Feints: ill omens
Filial: with the feelings of a son
Fliners: smithereens
Forfeiture: money that must be paid out to honour a guarantee

Galant: fashionable young man
Gallanting: behaving like fashionable, young lovers
Galled: chafe or rub sore
Garr'd: made
Giaours: eastern soldiers
Glasses: telescopes, binoculars
Goodman: husband or betrothed
Gossameres: thin threads
Greaves: leg armour
Ground-wa' stane: level of a building near to the ground
Gules: heraldic term for red
Gyse: manner

Hail'd: rain down blows
Hald: place of shelter
Hatchway: covering over an entry hole in the deck of a ship
Hoary: white and cold
Houri: dancing girl

Ignominy: dishonour

Ilk: each
Ilka tett: each tuft
Imag'ries: figures, representations
Imperious: mastering
Incredulous: disbelieving
Ingle-side: fireside
It winna ride: cannot be crossed: literally, won't take a man on horseback

Jacinth-work: inlay in semi-precious stone
Jargoning: singing
Jimp: graceful

Kems: combs
Kirk: chapel or church
Kites: birds of prey

'La belle dame sans mercy': the beautiful but cruel lady
Laith: loath
Land-sergeant: officer of the border watch
Lief: willing, prefer
Liege lord: a nobleman to whom duty is owed
line: equator
Louns: peasants, rogues
Louted: bowed
Lucent: shining
Lustrous: shining
Lute: a stringed musical instrument like a guitar

Mart: market
Martinmas: 11 November
Maudlin: self-indulgently despairing
Mauna: must not
Mese: alleviate
Mickle: much
Mien: bearing

Minion: effeminate youth
Mirk: dark
Minstrelsy: musicians
Missal: prayer book
Morphean: relating to Morpheus, the god of sleep
Multiplex: taking many forms

Neap: the tide at which the high water mark is lowest
Nogs: projecting pegs

Ousen: oxen
Outrageous: violent, cruel, immoral, abusive
Ower: before
Ower laigh: too short

Palsied: suffering from palsy, a disease which causes shaking fits
Parish-boys: orphans looked after in a charitable foundation
Pastoral: relating to the countryside
Patrimonial: inherited
Peerless: without equal
Phial: a small container for valuable liquids
Pinion: wing
Plummet: a lead weight
Poppied: drugged, as with opium
Post-boy: one who helps drive the horses of a coach, a postillion
Prate: talk idly
Prelude: a piece of music
Puir: poor

Rafted spirit: soul on its journey to eternity
Reek: smoke
Rhenish: wine
Rosary: a loop of beads whose differing sizes or spacings prompt those who are praying to say certain prayers

Sacrilegious: against the laws of God, the Bible and the Church
Saddle-tree: frame of a saddle
Sagacious: wise
Samite: rich silk fabric
Seraph: angel
Shrieve: to confess and purge away sin
Sic: such
Silly: having no feelings or intentions
Sma': little
Soldan: Sultan
Spouts: floods
Stane: stone
Stern: star
Stripling: a boy or youth
Supine: lying down
Supplications: begging for mercy
Surety: guarantee
Swound: dream

Tambour frame: a device for holding a piece of embroidery in while it is being worked
Timbrel: tambourine
Tolbooth: gaol
Tow: let down on a rope
Train-band: a troop of soldiers raised at the expense of the wealthier London citizens
Trig: trim
Troubadour: minstrel, a maker of music and song
Tuckets: calls on small trumpets
Turnpike: a gate across a main road opened for a fee which went towards maintenance

Unbodied: ghostlike, having no substance

Uncouth: rough, simple

Vaunts: boasts
verily: truly
Vermeil: vermilion, red
Vespers: evening prayers
Vivat Hispania: Long live Spain

Wan: pallid
Wae worth: woe to be
Wantonlie: alluring, lascivious
Waterflags: irises

Weird: fate
Wiles: tricks
Winsomely: charmingly
Wist: believe or think, or to know
Woofèd: thickly woven
Workhouse: a charitable home for the poor
Wrang: ?? *Yates:* gates

Yestreen: last evening

Examination Questions

1. Read the following passage, and answer **all** the questions printed beneath it:

> The Sun now rose upon the right:
> Out of the sea came he,
> Still hid in mist, and on the left
> Went down into the sea.
>
> And the good south wind still blew behind,   5
> But no sweet bird did follow,
> Nor any day for food or play
> Came to the mariners' hollo!
>
> And I had done a hellish thing,
> And it would work 'em woe: 10
> For all averred, I had killed the bird
> That made the breeze to blow.
> Ah wretch! said they, the bird to slay,
> That made the breeze to blow!
>
> Nor dim nor red, like God's own head,   15
> The glorious Sun uprist:
> Then all averred, I had killed the bird
> That brought the fog and mist.
> 'Twas right, said they, such birds to slay,
> That bring the fog and mist.   20
>
> The fair breeze blew, the white foam flew,
> The furrow followed free;
> We were the first that ever burst
> Into that silent sea.

> Down dropt the breeze, the sails dropt down,   25
> 'Twas sad as sad could be;
> And we did speak only to break
> The silence of the sea!

(i) In which direction is the ship travelling, and how can you tell this from the first stanza of this extract?

(ii) Explain *no sweet ... mariners' hollo!* (lines 6–8) and *And I had ... work 'em woe* (lines 9–10).

(iii) Comment on the effectiveness of lines 21–24 (*The fair breeze ... silent sea*).

(iv) Explain the changing attitudes of the Ancient Mariner's shipmates, as revealed in this extract.

(Oxford Local Examinations, 1982)

2. Read the following passage and answer the questions below it.

> Now lived the youth in freedom, but debarr'd
> From constant pleasure, and he thought it hard;
> Hard that he could not every wish obey,
> But must awhile relinquish ale and play;
> Hard! that he could not to his cards attend,
> But must acquire the money he would spend.
>
> With greedy eye he lood'd on all he saw,
> He knew not justice, and he laugh'd at law.
> On all he mark'd, he stretched his ready hand;
> He fish'd by water and he filch'd by land:
> Oft in the night has Peter dropp'd his oar,
> Fled from his boat, and sought for prey on shore;
> Of up the hedge-row glided, on his back
> Bearing the orchard's produce in a sack,
> Or farm-yard load, tugg'd fiercely from the stack;
> And as these wrongs to greater numbers rose,
> The more he look'd on all men as his foes.
>
> He built a mud-wall'd hovel, where he kept
> His various wealth, and there he oft-times slept;
> But no success could please his cruel soul.

(*a*) Choose three expressions from the passage which seem to you particularly effective and give reasons for your choice.

(*b*) Write an account of Peter's childhood and of his reaction to his father's death.

(*c*) Give a detailed account of the life of Peter's first apprentice and of the townspeople's reactions to Peter's treatment of him.

3. What characteristics of the Old Ballads do you consider appeal to modern readers? Illustrate your answer from at least two of the selected ballads.

(*University of London Examination Board, 1975*)

4. Read the following passage, and answer the questions printed beneath it:

> He follow'd through a lowly arched way,
> Brushing the cobwebs with his lofty plume,
> And as she mutter'd 'Well-a—well-a-day!'
> He found him in a little moonlight room,
> Pale, lattic'd, chill, and silent as a tomb. 5
> 'Now tell me where is Madeline,' said he,
> 'O tell me, Angela, by the holy loom
> 'Which none but secret sisterhood may see,
> 'When they St. Agnes' wool are weaving piously.'
>
> 'St. Agnes! Ah! it is St. Agnes' Eve— 10
> 'Yet men will murder upon holy days:
> 'Thou must hold water in a witch's sieve,
> 'And be liege-lord of all the Elves and Fays,
> 'To venture so: it fills me with amaze
> 'To see thee, Porphyro!—St. Agnes' Eve! 15
> 'God's help! my lady fair the conjuror plays
> 'This very night: good angels her deceive!
> 'But let me laugh awhile, I've mickle time to grieve.'

>   Feebly she laugheth in the languid moon,
>   While Porphyro upon her face doth look, 20
>   Like puzzled urchin on an aged crone
>   Who keepeth clos'd a wondrous riddle-book,
>   As spectacled she sits in chimney nook.
>   But soon his eyes grew brilliant, when she told
>   His lady's purpose; and he scarce could brook 25
>   Tears, at the thought of those enchantments cold,
>   And Madeline asleep in lap of legends old.

(i) Explain the meaning of *O tell me, Angela ... weaving piously* (lines 7–9); *hold water in a witch's sieve* (line 12); and *my lady fair the conjuror plays This very night* (lines 16–17).

(ii) What feelings does Angela show in this extract? From your knowledge of the poem as a whole, explain the reasons for these feelings as fully as you can.

(Oxford Local Examinations, 1980)

5. Comment on the effectiveness of the descriptions in both *Peter Grimes* and *The Ancient Marinewr*.

(University of London Examination Board, 1983)

6. Of the poems you have read for this examination which *two* have given you the most pleasure? Indicate why you enjoy them and comment on the way in which they are written.

(University of London Examination Board, 1983)

7. Give an account of *two* poems in which the poet has evoked a sense of mystery or of a supernatural presence.

(University of London Examination Board, 1983)

8. With reference to at least *two* poems show how you have been made more aware of some aspects of town life or country life.

(University of London Examination Board, 1983)